KEEP IT!

ADVANCED TAX
STRATEGIES FOR IRAS

KEEP IT!

ADVANCED TAX STRATEGIES FOR IRAs

POWERFUL WAYS TO PROTECT
YOUR IRA AND KEEP YOUR PIECE OF
THE $10 TRILLION DOLLAR PIE!

BY

JOE LUBY

Published By
West Lakes, LLC
1055 Whitney Ranch Drive
Suite 110
Henderson, NV 89014

First Edition.

ISBN - 13: 978-0615541334

This book is dedicated to my father, Joe O. Luby Jr., the best tax mind in the United States. May I enjoy half as much success in the individual tax realm as you have in the corporate world.

And to my son, Jack. May I leave you (a very long time from now!) an IRA large enough to benefit from the strategies presented herein.

Contents

Part Four: Creditor Protection & Bankruptcy

Part Five

Core Concepts

Introduction

The $3 Trillion Tax

The U.S. Federal Government has an almost $10 trillion savings account set aside that will produce roughly $3 trillion of income in the form of tax revenue. And you probably helped Uncle Sam build up this account by contributing to your IRA, 401(k) and other retirement plans over the years. The government is your silent (mostly) partner in these accounts.

It's like a farming partnership where you till the soil, plant the seeds, water the garden, pull the weeds, fertilize it and tend it every way necessary to produce a healthy crop. When it's time to enjoy the fruits of your labor, the tax man shows up and fills his truck with about a third of the total harvest.

Your silent partner did contribute some to the garden's success. Uncle Sam lent some of the seeds to be planted by allowing tax deductions on retirement plan contributions. And the government lets the crop grow to full maturity rather than pruning it back annually. They accomplish this by not taxing the earnings inside the account from year to year. The tax may not be due today, but it is due eventually.

Back to the $10 trillion. Where is all this money? The Investment Company Institute (www.ici.org) maintains ongoing research and statistics of the retirement plan market in the United States and produces a quarterly updated report. As of March 31st, 2011, IRA assets totaled $4.9 trillion. Defined contribution plans (also called DC plans) such as 401(k) and profit-sharing plans held another $4.7 trillion. I include DC plan assets since the vast majority of those dollars will eventually be rolled over into IRAs when the employees retire or change jobs.

Ninety-four percent of these dollars will be subject to tax upon withdrawal by the account owners! The other six percent is held in Roth IRAs that are generally non-taxable upon distribution which we'll discuss in more detail later.

As of this writing, the highest federal income tax bracket is thirty-five percent and scheduled to increase to thirty-nine point six percent (39.6%) in less than two years. The highest federal estate tax bracket is thirty-five percent and scheduled to increase to fifty-five percent in less than two years. So as mentioned, Uncle Sam stands to rake in a very hefty sum as these accounts get withdrawn and the owners pass away.

The estimated $3 trillion of tax revenue shown in the first paragraph assumes the government only gets an average of thirty percent of the total account values. As we will see, it can be a lot more in many cases.

Additionally, all levels of government are very hungry for more tax dollars right now. The IRS has become increasingly aggressive in audits and collections and has added many new agents in the last few years. The debate continues in Washington D.C. over whether and how much to raise taxes. The U.S. Government spends significantly more than it takes in each year. It is trillions of dollars in debt and looking for ways to increase income (tax revenue). Such a combination of factors is all but guaranteed to result in higher taxes going forward.

IRA owners need to be even more vigilant in seeking and implementing strategies to protect their nest eggs from the coming tax bite. Many people pay more than they need to simply because they don't know all the options available to them.

How to Use This Book

<u>IRA Owners:</u> The strategies described in this book will help you, and your family, pay the lowest amount of tax legally possible under the IRA rules.

Read the book straight through at first. The discussion in the later chapters builds on the material in the previous chapters, so jumping ahead can be confusing because the text references concepts explained in detail earlier in the book.

Then go back and review, make notes, highlight, dog ear and mark sections and strategies of interest. Compare the assets in your IRA to those discussed here. Offer a copy of this book to your professional advisor(s) if they are not familiar with some of the strategies presented that may be applicable or of interest to you.

<u>Professional Advisors (Attorneys, CPAs, Financial Advisors, etc.):</u> You will be able to apply these strategies with your clients immediately. You will also be able to use this knowledge to gain additional clients with large IRAs that can benefit from these advanced planning techniques.

Read through the material making notes of existing clients that may already fit some of the scenarios described. Consider the current asset mix held in your clients' IRAs and whether the strategies outlined here might apply. If not, consider what adjustments may be appropriate and in line with each client's overall planning goals.

Consider providing copies of this book to clients that can benefit from the strategies presented. You may also want to provide copies to prospects and centers of influence that you work with.

What You Will Learn

This book contains detailed analysis of some of the most powerful tax reduction strategies available for retirement account owners. The discussion revolves around traditional IRAs and Roth IRAs. Most defined contribution (profit-sharing plans, 401(k) plans, etc.) and even some defined benefit plan (pension plan) money eventually ends up in IRAs via rollovers at retirement or job change. Some of the strategies presented may have applications in those other plan types. However, this book does not address those situations or the differences that apply.

Part One outlines the core concepts that will be applied in the later sections.

Part Two highlights specific strategies involving the proper valuation of assets and utilizing appropriate valuation adjustments on assets held in IRAs. Most IRA owners and their advisors never give a passing thought to the valuation of assets held by the IRA. IRAs usually hold marketable securities such as publicly traded stocks, bonds, mutual funds, ETFs, money market funds, CDs and annuities. Thus whatever value is reported on the account statement is the accurate fair market value (FMV) of the IRA for tax purposes.

Other types of assets held by IRAs, such as real estate, partnerships, hedge funds, interval funds, private investment funds (PIFs), non-traded real estate investment trusts (REITs) and others, are more difficult to value properly. These assets generally do not trade daily like a stock or mutual fund and thus do not have readily available price quotations. The FMV of these holdings must be determined by an appraiser qualified to formulate opinions of value for each specific asset. This can offer significant tax advantages on a wide variety of IRA transactions.

Part Three outlines a series of strategies involving the use of leverage by an IRA. IRAs can borrow money for investment purposes just like an individual or other entity. There are certain criteria that must be followed within the IRA rules that are outlined here. Combining leverage with valuation adjustment strategies increases the tax savings opportunities exponentially.

Part Four contains discussion and strategies related to creditor protection of IRAs. The discussion includes examples pertaining to bankruptcy as well as general creditor protection (civil lawsuits, etc.).

Part Five has a variety of items to further your knowledge and learning. They include the conclusion, various appendices with additional information and resources, an index for easy reference when reviewing pertinent issues from the book and more.

Special Note:

Some people reading this book may be familiar with some of the strategies presented and may have already incorporated them into their own or client scenarios. Others, learning of them for the first time, will immediately recognize many opportunities for themselves and/or their clients. And a small minority of readers will declare the tax savings opportunities presented "too good to be true." Those readers will be glad to know I wrote a chapter specifically for them appropriately titled "Too Good to Be True." The chapter highlights common examples where the strategies outlined in this book are already being automatically applied by IRA custodians in order to maintain compliance with their industry rules and IRS regulations.

This book has more than one hundred footnotes with references to code sections, regulations, IRS publications, professional organizations, research and more. I encourage you to review the reference materials and consult with other professional advisors as part of your research. Tax laws change regularly, so you must come to your own conclusions based on the law in effect at any given time. This book is neither intended nor to be construed as tax, legal or investment advice.

Chapter One

IRA Investment Options

K ey to understanding the many IRA tax savings opportunities outlined in this book is to understand the wide array of investment options for IRAs.

The majority of IRAs are invested in "traditional" financial instruments such as stocks, bonds, mutual funds, CDs and annuities. In fact, mutual funds alone accounted for nearly half of all IRA holdings as of 2010.[1]

Why such a large percentage concentrated in common financial instruments? The simple answer is that IRAs must be held by an authorized custodian. These are typically banks, brokerage houses, mutual fund companies and insurance companies (or entities owned/controlled by same).[2] Such firms are in the business of creating, marketing, selling, advising on and holding traditional financial instruments as listed above. Banks sell CDs. Insurance companies sell annuities. Mutual fund companies sell mutual funds. Brokerage houses sell stocks and bonds.

IRAs are simply another account type offered by these custodians. Their real business is related to selling traditional financial instruments which is how they are compensated. They often don't charge anything for the service of being custodian on an IRA. They make their revenue from the products bought, sold and held by the IRA.

---

[1] Investment Company Institute. 2011. "The U.S. Retirement Market, Fourth Quarter 2010" (April).

[2] IRC 408(a)(2) & 408(h)

AND THAT'S PERFECTLY OK!

Some people when talking about this issue tend to demonize these IRA custodians as though making money from traditional financial instruments is bad. There is nothing wrong with it at all. It is simply a fact that because those custodial firms hold the majority of IRAs, the majority of assets held in IRAs are common financial products.

Yet IRA investors have a wide array of investment options available to them under the law. IRAs can invest in almost anything. An IRA is considered a trust for purposes of the tax code.[3] Just as other types of trusts can invest in many different types of assets, so too can IRAs.

Here are just a few examples of eligible IRA investments:

- Real estate (rentals, apartments, condos, raw land, office, industrial, etc.)
- Development projects
- Private equity
- Hedge funds
- Private investment funds (PIFs)
- Private Real Estate Investment Trusts (REITs)
- Small business start-ups
- Tax liens
- Options
- Promissory notes
- International real estate
- Precious metals (within certain guidelines referenced in Chapter Two)
- Trust deeds
- And more!

---

[3] IRC 408(a); Note: all references to "tax code" refer to the Internal Revenue Code of 1986, as amended from time to time.

In fact, many of the traditional custodians will act as custodian on these "alternative" assets. For example, an IRA can invest in a hedge fund or private REIT through most typical brokerage firms. Some banks (or their trust departments) will act as custodian on real estate transactions in IRAs.

In other cases, IRAs can be held at any of the top quality self-directed IRA custodians. Self-directed is a term of art in the industry, not a specific type of IRA. The term is not found in the tax code. It simply refers to an IRA held at a custodian that allows the IRA owner to self-direct the investments into any eligible asset. This includes traditional financial products in addition to the types of assets listed on page eighteen.

Self-directed custodians ONLY hold and report on the assets as required by the tax code. They do not provide investment advice or recommendations. They do not sell financial products or receive monies from the sale of such products. As such, custodial fees at these firms tend to be higher than mutual fund companies and other custodians. This is because the IRA owner is paying for pure custodial services.

Some traditional custodians such as brokerage firms even have relationships with one or more self-directed IRA custodians allowing the best of both worlds. Traditional IRA assets remain at the brokerage firm while alternative assets are held at the self-directed custodian. These arrangements often allow all the assets to be conveniently reported on one account statement.

For maximum cost effectiveness and convenience, you should usually hold traditional investments and "popular" alternative investments (see Chapter Five for examples and more information on these assets) at traditional custodians, and hold other alternative assets at self-directed custodians.

Chapter Two

Prohibited
Investments & Transactions

(WARNING:
Lots of tax code quotations just ahead!)

While the list of possible investment opportunities is very long, there are a few notable exceptions that must be reviewed. IRAs cannot do the following:

1. IRAs may not invest in life insurance contracts.[1]
2. IRAs may not invest in collectibles. An exception is made for certain precious metals in specific coin and/or bullion form.[2]
3. IRAs may not invest in stock of S-corporations.[3]
4. IRAs may not be pledged as security for a personal loan by the IRA owner.[4]
5. IRAs may not engage in prohibited transactions.[5]

The first four are fairly straightforward. Don't buy life insurance, S-corporation stock or collectibles with IRA money and don't pledge the account as collateral on a personal loan. No problem.

---

[1] IRC 408(a)(3)

[2] IRC 408(m)

[3] IRC 1361(b); Treasury Regulations 1.1361-1(h)(1)(vii)

[4] IRC 408(e)(4)

[5] IRC 4975(c)(1) and 408(e)(2)

The fifth one causes ulcers. What is a prohibited transaction (PT)? Here is the language right from the tax code:

4975(c) Prohibited transaction
> *(1) General rule*

For purposes of this section, the term "prohibited transaction" means any direct or indirect—
> *(A) sale or exchange, or leasing, of any property between a plan and a disqualified person;*
> *(B) lending of money or other extension of credit between a plan and a disqualified person;*
> *(C) furnishing of goods, services, or facilities between a plan and a disqualified person;*
> *(D) transfer to, or use by or for the benefit of, a disqualified person of the income or assets of a plan;*
> *(E) act by a disqualified person who is a fiduciary whereby he deals with the income or assets of a plan in his own interests or for his own account; or*
> *(F) receipt of any consideration for his own personal account by any disqualified person who is a fiduciary from any party dealing with the plan in connection with a transaction involving the income or assets of the plan.*

You probably noticed that several of the items listed refer to transactions between the IRA and a disqualified person. Who or what is a disqualified person? Here is the definition straight from the tax code:[6]

4975(e) Definitions
> *(2) Disqualified person*

---

[6] Note that certain definitions of disqualified persons are further affected by IRC sections 4975(e)(4) & (5) which invoke various constructive ownership and attribution rules generally found in IRC section 267(c). These rules can be very complicated and require careful examination by qualified professionals to ensure proper compliance.

For purposes of this section, the term "disqualified person" means a person who is—

 (A) a fiduciary;

 (B) a person providing services to the plan;

 (C) an employer any of whose employees are covered by the plan;

 (D) an employee organization any of whose members are covered by the plan;

 (E) an owner, direct or indirect, of 50 percent or more of—

  (i) the combined voting power of all classes of stock entitled to vote or the total value of shares of all classes of stock of a corporation,

  (ii) the capital interest or the profits interest of a partnership, or

  (iii) the beneficial interest of a trust or unincorporated enterprise,

  which is an employer or an employee organization described in subparagraph (C) or (D);

 (F) a member of the family (as defined in paragraph (6)) of any individual described in subparagraph (A), (B), (C), or (E);

 (G) a corporation, partnership, or trust or estate of which (or in which) 50 percent or more of—

  (i) the combined voting power of all classes of stock entitled to vote or the total value of shares of all classes of stock of such corporation,

  (ii) the capital interest or profits interest of such partnership, or

  (iii) the beneficial interest of such trust or estate,

  is owned directly or indirectly, or held by persons described in subparagraph (A), (B), (C), (D), or (E);

 (H) an officer, director (or an individual having powers or responsibilities similar to those of officers or directors), a 10 percent or more shareholder, or a highly compensated employee (earning 10 percent or more of

the yearly wages of an employer) of a person described in subparagraph (C), (D), (E), or (G); or (I) a 10 percent or more (in capital or profits) partner or joint venturer of a person described in subparagraph (C), (D), (E), or (G).

The Secretary, after consultation and coordination with the Secretary of Labor or his delegate, may by regulation prescribe a percentage lower than 50 percent for subparagraphs (E) and (G) and lower than 10 percent for subparagraphs (H) and (I).

Section F references any "member of the family" of the IRA owner. The tax code defines family member in this circumstance as:

(6) Member of family
For purposes of paragraph (2)(F), the family of any individual shall include his spouse, ancestor, lineal descendant, and any spouse of a lineal descendant.

In a nutshell, your IRA can't engage in any kind of dealings with a disqualified person. Here are a couple of simple examples:

Case Study – Bill's IRA Buys a Condo for His College Bound Daughter to Live in

Bill's daughter Amy is headed off to college out of state. Bill wants to buy a condo with his IRA in the city where Amy will be going to school and have Amy live in it. This is a PT because Bill's IRA is not allowed to furnish "goods, services or facilities" to Amy since she is a disqualified person. And before you ask, yes, it's still a PT even if Amy pays market rate rent to the IRA! Just see paragraph (A) from the prohibited transaction list shown earlier.

Case Study – Mark's IRA Owns an Office Building and Offers to Lease Space to Mark's Dental Practice

Mark's IRA owns a large mixed use building with vacant space that would be perfect for Mark's dental practice. The dental practice is structured as a corporation, and Mark owns seventy percent of the stock. Mark would like the dental corporation to rent space in the IRA-owned building. This is a PT because the dental corporation is a disqualified person with respect to Mark's IRA since he owns more than fifty percent of the stock.

The penalty for an IRA engaging in a prohibited transaction with either the owner or a beneficiary is the account ceases to be an IRA.[7] All assets are deemed to be distributed as of January 1st the same year the PT occurred and thus subject to tax, and possibly penalty, depending on circumstances.[8]

In very broad terms, make sure all IRA transactions are truly arms-length investment deals between neutral third parties. The intricate details, nuances and possibilities of PTs are beyond the scope of this book. This is an area where expert advice should be sought on a per transaction basis. Don't gamble with PTs and hope you get it right. Get quality professional advice to be certain. The cost of losing IRA status, paying taxes and possibly penalties is too high when there are professionals that specialize in this area and can steer you clear of the problem areas.

---

[7] IRC 408(e)(2)(A)

[8] IRC 408(e)(2)(B)

Chapter Three

Valuation of IRA Assets

The total value of all assets held by an IRA is important at specific times for specific reasons. They are:

1. Anytime a taxable or potentially taxable event occurs (distributions, Roth conversions, rollovers, early withdrawals, etc.).
2. Annually on December 31st beginning the year before the IRA owner turns age 70 ½ in order to calculate correct required minimum distributions (RMDs).
3. Date of IRA owner's death, or alternate valuation date six months later, for calculating the gross estate for estate tax purposes.[1]
4. In the case of bankruptcy of the IRA owner to determine how much of the IRA may be protected under the bankruptcy rules.
5. In the case of lawsuit/judgment against the IRA owner to determine how much of the IRA may be protected under state law.

The rest of the time, *for tax purposes at least*, the value of an IRA is essentially meaningless. Even the IRS agrees that valuation is not as important when there is no taxable event. Consider the following quote from the IRS' own instruction manual:

> "Whether a formal valuation is required will depend on the transactions that occur with the

---

[1] IRC 2032

plan and the form of the plan. For example, the valuation in a single participant plan, a self-directed account, or frozen plan can be less formal in a year in which the plan or self-directed account receives no contribution and makes no distribution or change in investment."[2]

For example, Susan's traditional IRA has investments worth $25,000. Ten years later she closes the IRA withdrawing all the assets with no other transactions having occurred during that time. The total account value is $50,000 at the time of distribution. Susan's custodian reports the value on Form 1099-R, and she recognizes this amount as taxable income in the year of distribution.[3] The value of the IRA only truly matters in this scenario at the time of distribution because it is a taxable event. Proper valuation is required to determine the correct amount of income to report and thus the appropriate tax owed.

The account statement could reflect $25 or $2,500,000 for the entire ten year period when no taxable event occurred. The value reported on Susan's account statement is completely irrelevant with no effect whatsoever until a taxable event occurs. Of course, Susan wants accurate values reported during the interim period for her own personal uses such as determining investment performance, net worth, etc. She would also want accurate values reported for the purposes described in Part Four of this book. And the IRA rules require accurate interim reporting as shown in the next section. But from a technical standpoint with regard to determining taxable income, interim valuation matters not one whit.

---

[2]   Internal Revenue Manual section 4.72.8.1.2 related to "valuing assets in a qualified retirement plan."

[3]   IRC 408(d)(1); Treasury Regulations Section 1.408-7

What Value Does the Law Require?

The law is very clear on what value must be used when calculating RMDs, reporting distributions or other taxable events and retirement plan situations. Fair market value (FMV) is the required valuation.[4]

IRA custodians are required to report the December 31st FMV of an IRA to both the owner and the IRS annually.[5] The report to the IRS is made via Form 5498. The IRS instructions on how to properly complete Form 5498 read in part:

> "Box 5. Fair market value of account
> Enter the FMV of the account on December 31.
> For inherited IRAs, see Inherited IRAs on page 16.
>
> *Caution: Trustees and custodians are responsible for ensuring that all IRA assets (including those not traded on established markets or with otherwise readily determinable market value) are valued annually at their fair market value.*"[6]
> [Emphasis in the original.]

---

[4] Note that valuation references not intended to be an exhaustive list: Treasury Regulations Sections 1.402(a)-1(a)(1)(iii), 1.408-4(c)(2)(iii), 1.408-4(d)(1), 1.408-6(d)(4)(iii)(B)(1), 1.408-6(d)(4)(iii)(B)(2), 1.408A-4, A-14, 1.408A-5-A-2(c)(3), 1.408A-6, A-16, 1.412(c)(2)-1(c)(1); Notice 89-25, 1989-1 C.B. 662, A-10; Preamble to TD 9220, 8-19-2005; IRS *2011 Instructions for Forms 1099-R and 5498*, pgs. 8 & 18; Internal Revenue Manual sections 4.72.8.1, 4.72.8.4; IRC Sections 408(e)(2)(B), 408(e)(3), 414(I)(2)(C), 4973(a), 4975(f)(4)

[5] IRC 408(i); Treasury Regulations Section 1.408-5

[6] IRS *2011 Instructions for Forms 1099-R and 5498*, pg. 18

The same IRS document contains the instructions to custodians on how to complete Form 1099-R which is required to report IRA distributions, Roth conversions and other retirement plan transactions. Those instructions read in part:

> "Box 1. Gross Distribution
> Employer Securities and other property.
> If you distribute employer securities or other property, include in box 1 the FMV of the securities or other property on the date of distribution."[7]

"Other property" in this section refers to in-kind distributions of property other than cash. FMV is easy to determine on assets "traded on established markets or with otherwise readily determinable market value." One simply looks up the current trading price of the asset. For example, publicly traded stocks, bonds, mutual funds, ETFs, precious metals, commodities, and more all have a readily determinable FMV. These assets are traded daily with up to the second pricing information and generally full liquidity.

What about assets that are not traded openly on an established exchange? Determining FMV for assets that do not have a ready market of buyers and sellers requires a little more effort. Specifically, it requires a qualified appraiser to evaluate the asset in detail and provide a report of their expert opinion of FMV if the asset were to be sold.

The standard used is called the "willing buyer, willing seller" rule. The definition reads as follows:

---

[7] IRS *2011 Instructions for Forms 1099-R and 5498*, pg. 8

"The price at which the property would change hands between a willing buyer and a willing seller, neither being under any compulsion to buy or sell and both having reasonable knowledge of the relevant facts."[8]

The appraiser must look at all the variables and details of the asset in question and place themselves in the shoes of the hypothetical willing buyer and willing seller to determine an appropriate FMV. For business interests, they will review the industry, the company's position amongst its competitors, the ownership structure and agreements, gross/net profit history and projections, etc.

An everyday example is found in the real estate market. Buyers typically hire an appraiser to provide a valuation report prior to closing a deal. Lenders require appraisals before finalizing loans and will sometimes cancel a loan due to a lower than expected valuation. These appraisals are required because real estate is illiquid and does not have readily available price quotations. To determine what a property is worth, a qualified appraiser must review specific and pertinent details such as:

- Location
- Size
- Improvements on the property
- Zoning and current usage
- Similar properties on the market
- Recent transactions involving similar properties
- Current demand for such properties

---

[8] Treasury Regulations Sections 25.2512-1, 20.2031-1(b), 1.412(c)(2)-1(c)(1); Revenue Ruling 59-60, 1959-1 C.B. 237

The valuation method used by an appraiser will vary depending on the type of asset at hand. The reported FMV will also vary dramatically, even between two seemingly similar assets, based on the multitude of details and information that go into a professional valuation engagement.

Chapter Four

Valuation Adjustments

Valuation adjustment factors cause a difference between a particular asset's net asset value (NAV) and its FMV. Adjustment factors may cause an increase or decrease in the FMV depending on circumstances.

Valuation adjustment factors that cause a decrease in FMV from NAV are generally referred to as "discounting factors" or simply "discounts." Most strategies used by tax planners are designed to specifically cause a decrease in FMV of a particular asset or group of assets. Thus discounting techniques are very common in a wide variety of tax planning scenarios.

The reasoning is straightforward: in most taxable transactions, the lower the value involved, the less tax is owed. For example, a father making a gift of 1,000 shares of Coca-Cola stock to his son would incur gift tax based on the total FMV of the shares.[1] A low share price on the stock at the time of the gift results in less gift tax owed on the transaction.

The following are common valuation adjustment factors that can cause an asset to reflect a FMV lower than its NAV:

Lack of Control (Minority Interest): Refers to situations where the interest to be valued represents a less than controlling interest in the overall asset. For example, a ten percent interest in a company or partnership would generally be a minority interest lacking a controlling vote.

---

[1] Assumes annual gift tax exclusion and lifetime gift tax exemption do not apply.

Lack of Marketability: Assets that are not able to be bought and sold readily on established exchanges are generally said to suffer from a lack of marketability. They do not have a ready market of buyers and sellers.

Lack of Liquidity: Assets that do not provide cash flow to the investor such as dividends, interest payments, profit or other cash distributions. Such assets are held purely for capital growth opportunities and often have very extended time horizons.

Blockage/Market Absorption: Refers to scenarios where selling a particular asset, or group of assets, would flood the market and cause a decrease in value for the asset(s). This is often applied to artwork, collectibles and real estate.

Restricted Securities Discount: Securities subject to transfer or trading restrictions for some period of time are subject to this discount.

Fractional Interest: Undivided fractional interests in real property cannot easily be sold and are generally subject to this discount.

Built-in Capital Gains: This factor generally pertains to C-corporations that hold assets with substantial unrealized capital gains. A new buyer of the corporation will eventually incur the tax on those gains and therefore demands a discount to reflect future tax liability.

Assignee Status: Recipients of transferred LP and LLC interests are usually not considered full substitute partners or members of the entity automatically. Instead they become assignees holding the economic benefits of ownership but not the voting and other management benefits of ownership.

Fiduciary Obligation: Situations where an owner of an asset has substantial fiduciary liability or obligation to the other owners can serve to reduce asset values due to this increased risk.

Portfolio Discount (undiversified/unattractive portfolio of assets): This factor refers to situations where a buyer may be purchasing a variety of assets within the same entity (LP, LLC, etc.) that may be unattractive in some aspects. For example, an entity holding a top quality bond portfolio that also includes a large block of non-performing notes may be subject to this factor.

Closed end mutual funds trading on an exchange are examples of where NAV and FMV are almost always different. The shares have a NAV based on the total underlying portfolio value of the fund which is calculated daily. However, FMV is the price at which the shares are trading on the exchange at any given moment and can vary widely throughout the day. Closed end fund shares trading at a price higher than the underlying NAV are said to be at a premium, and shares trading for less than NAV are said to be at a discount.

The following case study shows discounting principles at work in valuing a private non-traded business interest:

Case Study – Four Brothers Dry Cleaning, Inc.

Four Brothers Dry Cleaning, Inc. is a successful business with five locations in a large metropolitan area. The company was founded fifteen years ago by four college buddies that all belonged to the same fraternity – Joe, Kevin, Bill and Doug. The name "Four Brothers" stems from their college days as fraternity brothers.

The four owners are equal twenty-five percent shareholders, and the company has a book value of $10,000,000. Each owner's interest in the company is worth $2,500,000 on paper.

The company is privately held by the four friends, and there has never been a sale transaction involving company shares. Each owner has held his same one quarter interest since founding the company.

Kevin is forty years old and has decided to sell his interest in the company and pursue other endeavors. He must give the other three partners right of first refusal per their company agreement. They decline to purchase Kevin's shares, so he must find an outside buyer. There is no existing market for shares of the company, and Kevin does not have a ready and willing buyer to turn to right away. He hires a business broker to help locate a buyer. It takes several months of marketing to potential buyers before the broker finds an interested party.

A potential buyer named John is interested in the company for the future profit potential. He has done research into the dry cleaning industry and found that it can be very profitable but has never worked in or owned a dry cleaning business personally. He also doesn't know any of the current owners, did not attend the same university and was not a member of their fraternity.

Kevin listed his interest in the company for sale at the full book value of $2,500,000. John is willing to make an offer but not at the full asking price. After considerable negotiation Kevin and John agree to a sale price of $1,500,000. This represents a forty percent discount from book value (NAV) for Kevin's one quarter interest in the company. FMV of a twenty-five percent interest in Four Brothers Dry Cleaning, Inc. has now been established as $1,500,000 via a willing buyer and willing seller negotiating a price on fair terms.

Why did John insist on, and Kevin accept, such a large valuation adjustment from the book value of the shares? Let's review from both perspectives:

Kevin: Kevin had to list the asset with a broker and pay a commission along with a variety of legal and accounting expenses in order to sell his shares. He had to wait a significant amount of time (several months) before having the opportunity to convert his shares into cash. It was difficult to find a buyer in the first place, and Kevin didn't know when or if another likely buyer would come along. Kevin had to make the asset attractive to John to entice him to go through with the deal which equated to a lower price. Kevin was under pressure to get the shares sold to free up capital for other endeavors.

John: John had to consider a variety of issues in deciding on an agreeable purchase price. He knew even though the shares' book value (NAV) was $2.5 million, he could not convert the shares into $2.5 million cash any time he needed. The shares suffer from a lack of marketability. They are difficult to sell quickly because there is no ready market of buyers. John also knew he was buying a minority position and joining three partners that knew each other very well and had worked together for a long time. John could always be out voted. This creates a lack of control or minority interest discount issue. John also cannot force a dividend, salary, sale of assets or any other cash distribution or liquidation type event in order to generate cash from his shares. This creates a lack of liquidity John must be prepared to endure indefinitely. He cannot control the future direction of the company or sway future actions by the board creating inherent risk to his capital investment.

Assets Subject to Valuation Adjustment/Discount

The following list shows examples of assets generally subject to the discounting principles. It is intended to show the wide range of assets subject to discounts and is by no means an exhaustive list of possibilities:

- Closely held C corporations
- S corporations
- Limited Liability Company (LLC) interests
- Limited Partnership (LP) interests
- Fractional ownership in real property
- Partial interests in real estate LPs/LLCs
- Private real estate investment trusts (REITs)
- Private investment funds (PIFs)
- Hedge funds
- Private equity (PE) funds
- Restricted stock
- Assignee interests
- Fine art collections
- Concentrated real estate portfolios
- Copyrighted works
- Patents
- Notes
- Illiquid fixed income securities
- Interval funds
- Closed end funds

Range of Discounts in Percentage Terms

Every case is different and every asset being evaluated by an appraiser is different. While there may be general similarities, the relevant factors will vary dramatically.

Consider a one acre parcel of vacant land. What is its FMV? If you can answer that accurately without additional information, quit reading this book and go make billions in the stock market or on the lottery. Of course, no one can answer the question of value for a one acre parcel of land without knowing more details. The major missing piece is: where is the acre of land? An acre of land in rural North Dakota will not fetch the same FMV as an acre of land in London or New York City.

Valuation adjustment percentages vary greatly. For example, a quick look at the twenty-five largest discounts found in closed end funds according to the Closed-End Fund Association's website as I write this shows a range of -13.89% to -42.68%.[2]

Table One shows a sample list of court cases in this area with the actual amount of discount applied to the assets. In each case, the asset being valued was ownership in some type of legal entity such as a limited partnership, limited liability company or corporation. The assets shown are just for reference and indicate the type of assets held inside the LP, LLC or corporation valued in that case.

Table 1

Knight	Securities/RE	15%
Dailey	Securities	40%
Adams	Securities/RE/Minerals	54%
Church	Securities/RE	63%
McCord	Securities/RE	32%
Lappo	Securities/RE	35.4%
Peracchio	Securities	29.5%
Deputy	Boat company	30%
Green	Bank stock	46%
Thompson	Publishing company	40.5%
Kelley	Cash	32%
Bergquist/Kendrick	Medical practice	64.25%
Litchfield I	Securities/RE	47.2%
Litchfield II	Securities	46.2%
Miller	Securities	35%
Pierre	Cash	36.5%
Keller	Securities	47.51%

[2] www.closed-endfunds.com

We look to past court cases for examples because it's the only opportunity to examine scenarios and see the actual discounts applied. Tax returns reflecting discounted assets which are not disputed are not subject to review by the public or planning community.

For example, Paul dies owning $6,000,000 of assets valued at NAV. The single largest holding is Paul's partial interest in the family business with a NAV of $3,000,000. Paul was one of six different family members holding stock in the company. Upon his death, an appraisal was conducted which determined the FMV of Paul's portion to be $1,800,000, a forty percent discount from NAV. Thus Paul's overall estate value for estate tax calculations is only $4,800,000, which is less than the current federal threshold where estate tax would apply. If this valuation is never challenged by the IRS in a public venue (i.e. via the court system) then only the family, their advisors and the IRS know the specific discount applied.

There are many top notch appraisers doing this type of work every day. They are very professional, often hold multiple credentials and many have testified in tax court about valuation issues. They give their honest evaluation of FMV taking into account all pertinent information, regardless of the reason for the appraisal request. For example, an estate may desire a very large discount applied to an asset in order to reduce estate tax owed. Another person may desire a large premium applied to an asset being donated to charity to support a large charitable tax deduction. In either case, the reason for the appraisal is irrelevant and does not affect valuation. A good appraiser will give the FMV as they see it whether it helps or hurts the person requesting the report. And that's how it should be. FMV is part science and part art, but never related to the final use of the appraisal report.

Chapter Five

Popular Alternative Investments

The term "alternative investment" means different things to different people. Generally, it's easier to describe what is not considered an alternative investment by the investment industry. Traditional assets such as publicly traded stocks, bonds, mutual funds, exchange traded funds, closed end funds, certificates of deposit, annuities and other similar investment vehicles are not considered alternative. Alternative investments are often described as anything other than the items on that list. Note that some alternative investments are only available to "accredited investors." Please see Appendix D for more information on this term.

Some of the most common and popular alternative investments are:

- Hedge funds
- Private investment funds (PIFs)
- Private/unlisted real estate investment trusts (REITs)
- Private equity funds
- Oil & Gas partnerships

Many brokerage and investment firms have entire marketing and advisory departments dedicated solely to the realm of alternative investments. They conduct due diligence on product sponsors and provide analysis for use by their financial advisors and clients. They also provide marketing and sales assistance to advisors working with individual clients that have interest in these products.

It is very common for portfolio recommendations from major

investment firms to suggest some percentage of client assets be invested in alternative investments. Alternative asset classes can provide valuable diversification to client portfolios. They also allow for a wider variety of investment styles and opportunities than traditional asset classes.

For example, consider the concept of a long/short equity hedge fund. Mutual fund managers are restricted by law on what type of assets they can hold, quantities of each, how much leverage they can use, the use of derivatives, liquidity requirements, etc. So the typical equity mutual fund buys and sells publicly traded stocks that fit the fund's investment mandate. Small cap funds buy small cap stocks, technology funds buy technology company stocks and so on. The goal of the manager is to buy a stock today and sell it in the future for a higher price (buy low and sell high). Investors in mutual funds are generally limited to returns generated by the manager successfully picking stocks that go up in value. However, fund managers are also able to make predictions of which stocks may go down in value. A manager looking at Shoe Company A and Shoe Company B might determine that Shoe Company A has great prospects while Shoe Company B is in terrible shape. So they buy shares of Shoe Company A for their mutual fund portfolio but cannot act on their research and predictions about Shoe Company B due to the fund restrictions.

In a long/short equity hedge fund, the manager can buy shares of Shoe Company A expecting them to increase in value. At the same time, he can sell shares of Shoe Company B short, expecting those shares to decrease in value.[1] In this scenario,

---

[1] Short selling is when shares are borrowed from a brokerage firm and sold on the open market at the current price. The trader expects the shares to decrease in value over time which will allow them to buy shares back at a reduced price and repay the loan from the brokerage firm. The risk is the shares may increase in value instead which forces the trader to buy them back at a higher price and lose money.

investors are benefitting from the manager's research and knowledge in both directions: on an asset he feels will go up in value and on one he feels will decrease in value. The manager has not done any different research or come to any different conclusions than he did when managing the mutual fund, except now he can potentially create better returns by making trades in both companies.

This is just one example of one type of hedge fund. Hedge funds come in all shapes, sizes and flavors. There are event driven funds, merger arbitrage funds and multi-strategy funds among many others. There are even hedge fund-of-funds which are hedge funds that hold a portfolio of other hedge funds. They are designed to provide diversification and professional oversight of multiple hedge fund positions.

Private REITs, also called "unlisted REITS", are very popular assets that allow investors to gain exposure to many different sectors of the large scale commercial real estate world with relatively low initial investments. Some REITs focus on very specific sectors of the real estate market such as apartments, industrial, office buildings, storage facilities, shopping centers, etc. Others focus on specific geographic regions and some are more broadly diversified into different property types. Private REIT shares do not trade on public exchanges and are generally illiquid except for limited redemption programs offered by the REIT sponsors themselves. The goal of most private REITs is to build up their portfolios and eventually list their shares on a public exchange providing liquidity to investors. Private REITs have historically paid very high dividends making them particularly attractive investments to investors seeking income and cash flow.

Private investment funds often have similar investment objectives to traditional mutual funds. They are usually structured as limited partnerships or limited liability companies and have specific time horizons during which investors must remain fully invested. This design feature creates an automatic long-term investment outlook. It allows the fund managers to concentrate on investment opportunities and performance without worrying about redemptions out of the fund at inopportune times in their investment cycle. For example, assume the manager recently purchased shares of Widgets Inc. Her expectation is that Widgets Inc. will complete their new manufacturing facility and introduce a new line of widgets in two years that will greatly increase the stock value. In a mutual fund, the manager could face heavy investor redemptions out of the fund at any time causing her to liquidate part or all of the Widgets Inc. holdings prior to her target date. A PIF prevents this type of concern, and the manager can hold the stock as long as necessary within the PIF's designated time horizon. PIFs also generally allow investors access to institutional level portfolios, pricing, managers and opportunities normally unavailable to individuals with less than $5,000,000 to commit to a particular portfolio.

All of these alternative investments have similar characteristics that affect their FMV. Many of the valuation adjustment factors described in Chapter Four apply to these types of holdings. This is good news since many advisors already recommend and utilize these types of assets with their clients. They are also well established asset classes with billions (if not trillions) of investor dollars already invested. Thus, many investors may be able to take advantage of the transactions described in the next three sections of this book using assets they already hold in their IRAs. It also means investors that do not own these types of assets are likely to be able to find attractive alternative investment options that are well suited to their investment needs and time horizon.

PART TWO

IRA Transactions with Discounted Assets

Chapter Six

Opportunities for IRAs

What does all this mean for IRA investors?
Huge tax savings opportunities!

Many IRA transactions and their taxation are based on the FMV of IRA assets involved. These include:

- Distributions/withdrawals
- Roth conversions
- Required minimum distribution (RMD) calculations
- RMD value for tax reporting
- Stretch IRA RMDs
- Estate tax calculations

Therefore, just as in the example of the father gifting shares of Coca-Cola stock to his son, a reduced FMV serves to reduce the tax owed on the IRA transaction. A withdrawal of IRA assets with NAV of $100,000 and discounted FMV of $70,000 results in $70,000 of taxable income, not $100,000.

A reduction in IRA value due to holding discounted assets, also results in lower RMDs. Lower RMDs mean less income to report and lower tax bills. It also means the IRA will last longer since less money has to come out of the account each year.

Roth conversions are generally taxable events where the amount of income reported is based on the FMV of the traditional IRA at the time of conversion. Thus a lower FMV results in significant tax savings on Roth conversions.

In Chapter Four, we briefly reviewed how a reduced FMV can contribute to substantial estate tax savings. The same concept applies to discounted IRAs when calculating the gross estate for tax purposes. Inherited IRAs are also subject to RMDs that can often be stretched over the beneficiary's lifetime, hence the term "stretch-IRA." Reduced FMVs in these accounts help maintain more assets in the tax protected IRA during the life of the beneficiary.

This Part Two of the book highlights various opportunities to reduce tax impact on IRAs holding assets subject to valuation discounts. Another important non-tax opportunity for IRAs holding discounted assets is related to asset protection and bankruptcy. Please see Chapter Twenty-Six for more details on this.

NOTE: Almost every scenario throughout this book uses the same hypothetical valuation adjustment of thirty percent. Why? Because I made it up! When appropriate to the discussion, I made up other discount amounts also such as twenty-five and forty percent. There is no guarantee of a particular discount and as described earlier, there are adjustments upward and downward that may apply in any particular circumstance. So don't get hung up on the specific discount shown. I had to use something, and thirty percent sounded good. Thirty percent is also well within the range of actual discount examples shown in Chapter Four. Real adjustments will vary dramatically and may be significantly higher or lower. Additionally, the only way to know if a discount actually applies to a specific asset is to hire an appraiser to conduct a formal valuation analysis.

ANOTHER NOTE: Almost every case study and example uses one million dollars as the NAV of the assets involved. Yes, I made this up too! One million is an easy number to work with and keeps things interesting. It is not intended to imply the strategies only apply to very large IRAs. The concepts are the same regardless of the account values. Only the numbers and tax brackets will change from case to case.

Chapter Seven

Roth IRA Conversions

One of the most powerful applications of discount valuation principles is in the Roth conversion scenario. A Roth conversion is when a traditional IRA is converted into a Roth IRA. Generally, assets held in traditional IRAs are subject to ordinary income tax upon conversion or withdrawal.[1] The amount of income reported is equivalent to the FMV of the assets at the time of conversion.[2]

Roth IRAs are attractive accounts because they provide completely tax-free growth and distributions.[3] Converting a taxable traditional IRA to a Roth IRA is similar to paying tax on the seeds so the future harvest can be reaped tax-free.

Assume Mary converts her traditional IRA holding marketable securities and cash valued at $1,000,000 to a Roth IRA in 2011. Mary receives a Form 1099-R from her IRA custodian reflecting the full FMV of the converted assets as ordinary income for the 2011 tax year. Using a hypothetical combined federal and state tax bracket of forty percent, her total

---

[1] IRC Sections 408(d) & 408A(d)(3); Cumulative prior nondeductible contributions are not subject to tax upon withdrawal or conversion.

[2] See discussion and footnotes in Chapter Three.

[3] Roth IRA distributions are tax-free provided certain conditions are met [IRC 408A(d)]. There are circumstances which cause a Roth IRA to incur a tax on its earnings called the unrelated business income tax (UBIT). For more information on UBIT see Chapter Seventeen.

tax bill on the transaction is $400,000.[4] Ideally, Mary pays the tax with funds outside her IRA in order to maintain the large Roth IRA balance for future tax-free growth.

Table 2

Roth Conversion with Marketable Securities and/or Cash	
IRA Net Asset Value	$1,000,000
Qualified Appraiser's Discount	N/A
Fair Market Value of Conversion	$1,000,000
Tax on Conversion (assumed 40% tax bracket)	($400,000)

Some commentators downplay the Roth conversion opportunity because of the necessity of incurring a large tax bill early. A common argument is that clients may end up in a lower tax bracket in later years when withdrawing the IRA assets and thus should have waited instead of paying tax at a higher rate today. The opportunity cost of paying the tax upfront is also sometimes a concern.

However, these arguments fail to consider the impact of using discount valuation strategies prior to the Roth conversion. The result is a dramatically reduced effective tax rate on the transaction.

Consider the same transaction described above except now Mary's IRA holds a ten percent interest in an illiquid real estate

---

[4] The highest federal income tax bracket as of May 2011 is 35%. It is scheduled to increase to 39.6% on January 1, 2013. Most states also impose a state income tax.

limited partnership. A qualified appraisal of the IRA's minority interest in the LP determines a FMV of $700,000, a thirty percent discount from her $1,000,000 NAV. Mary executes a Roth IRA conversion, and the Form 1099-R received from her IRA custodian reflects the discounted FMV of the account at the time of conversion. Her taxable income from the transaction is $700,000 instead of $1,000,000. The tax bill is now only $280,000 using the same assumed forty percent combined federal and state tax bracket.

Table 3

Roth Conversion with Illiquid Alternative Asset(s)	
IRA Net Asset Value	$1,000,000
Qualified Appraiser's Discount[5]	30%
Fair Market Value of Conversion	$700,000
Tax on Conversion (assumed 40% tax bracket)	($280,000)

The tax owed on the exact same transaction with the exact same NAV is thirty percent less!

Mary saves $120,000 of tax on the transaction. That's a twelve percent "gain" on the $1,000,000 NAV of her IRA before any investment returns of the LP are considered.

The tax bill is equivalent to a combined twenty-eight percent effective tax rate based on the IRA's full NAV of $1,000,000. [6]

---

[5] Hypothetical discount used for illustrative purposes only. See note in Chapter six.

[6] $280,000 tax/$1,000,000 IRA NAV = 28% combined effective tax rate.

Someone that would not consider a Roth conversion based on a forty percent tax bracket may find it very attractive at a twenty-eight percent tax bracket. And it certainly deflates the argument that one is likely to be in a lower tax bracket when withdrawing IRA funds later in life.

Many individuals with significant assets, pensions, incomes, investment holdings and so on, are destined to always be in a high income tax bracket. Using our hypothetical example, the question is simply: will Mary's top tax bracket ever be less than twenty-eight percent? If the answer is safely assumed to be no, then the conversion makes sense because she will never have the opportunity to pay tax at such a low rate on these assets (plus all future growth post-conversion is tax-free no matter what bracket she is in later in life).

Another way to evaluate a Roth conversion scenario is to ask the following questions:

1. What does the tax bracket in retirement need to be to make holding the traditional IRA and paying tax upon withdrawal more attractive?
2. Is it likely that the IRA owner will ever be in that reduced bracket?

Here is a side-by-side comparison of the net results between holding a traditional IRA versus converting to Roth. The following assumptions apply in this analysis:

- Combined state and federal income tax bracket – 40%
- Traditional IRA NAV - $1,000,000
- Non-IRA assets available to pay tax on conversion - $280,000
- Valuation adjustment (discount) – 30%
- Annual growth rate on IRA assets – 8%

- Annual growth rate on non-IRA assets (reduced to account for taxes on portfolio) – 6%
- Time horizon to retirement/withdrawal – 10 years
- Numbers rounded to nearest $100

Table 4

	Traditional IRA	Roth Conversion
IRA NAV	$1,000,000	$1,000,000
Valuation Adjustment	N/A	30%
IRA FMV	$1,000,000	$700,000
Tax on Conversion (40%)	N/A	($280,000)
Net Non-IRA Assets	$280,000	N/A
Future NAV of IRA	$2,159,000	$2,159,000
Future NAV of non-IRA assets	$501,400	N/A
Tax on Withdrawal	($863,600)	N/A
Net remaining after tax	$1,796,800	$2,159,000
Net advantage of Roth IRA	--	**+$362,200**

In this scenario, the break even tax rate for the traditional IRA to match the net after tax result of the Roth IRA in retirement is twenty-three percent.[7] In other words, the traditional IRA dollars would have to be taxed at a rate of only twenty-three percent in order for the net remaining after tax to match the $2,159,000 net from the Roth conversion side of the table. Any rate higher than this and the Roth conversion strategy comes out ahead. And remember that is a combined state and federal tax rate.

Now we've determined the answer to question number one: twenty-three percent in this example. This number will change based on the particulars of the situation under review including assumptions applied. Question number two asks whether we believe the IRA owner will ever be in a lower tax bracket than twenty-three percent. For most investors with IRA assets, the answer is a resounding NO.

The gap becomes even wider as the assets remain in the Roth IRA for longer periods. For example, if we run the same numbers out twenty years, the combined tax bracket must be less than twenty percent to beat the Roth IRA outcome. Thus, Roth conversions are even better for those with extended time horizons before their IRA assets will be used. For families planning on long-term stretch IRA status (where distributions are stretched out over the longest possible time allowed under the rules based on a beneficiary life expectancy) the Roth IRA can transfer incredible amounts of tax-free wealth to the next generation.

---

[7] Rounded, actual rate is 23.22%.

Consider the current federal income tax brackets and the increases scheduled in 2013:[8]

Table 5

2011-2012 Federal Income Tax Brackets	2013+ Federal Income Tax Brackets
10%	--
15%	15%
25%	28%
28%	31%
33%	36%
35%	39.6%

Currently, only two brackets are below the breakeven point of twenty-three percent from the prior example. Starting January 1, 2013, only one bracket is less than the breakeven point. These are just the federal tax brackets and do not consider additional state income taxes where applicable. Given the budget concerns and issues going on at all levels of government in the United States, it is likely these rates will rise over time.

Again, one must ask: how likely is it that an IRA owner will EVER be in a tax bracket low enough to make holding their traditional IRA financially rewarding compared to a Roth conversion with discounted assets? The odds are very slim assuming they have some time between the conversion date and withdrawal date.

---

[8] The Tax Relief, Unemployment Insurance Reauthorization and Job Creation Act of 2010, signed into law December 17, 2010, extended the 2010 tax rates until January 1, 2013.

As with any investment, Mary assumes the risk of loss of principal. This is true regardless of the type of investment or whether she converts to a Roth IRA. Is converting to a Roth IRA and paying tax on the current value a good idea in the event her investment loses money? Assume Mary converted her $1,000,000 traditional IRA to a Roth IRA and paid tax on that amount. If the account later drops to $500,000 at the time of withdrawal, she is worse off than if she had just held the traditional IRA.[9] She would have been better off withdrawing $500,000 and paying tax on that amount rather than converting and paying tax on $1,000,000.

Holding discounted assets in the traditional IRA prior to conversion provides significant downside protection to her IRA in the event of an investment loss. She started with an IRA valued at $1,000,000 and ended up paying income tax on a Roth conversion value of only $700,000. The Roth IRA NAV could drop in value all the way to $700,000 before keeping the traditional IRA would have been more attractive tax-wise than the conversion. From a tax perspective, she gave herself $300,000 of downside protection.

Given a long enough time horizon, everyone assumes a positive return on invested assets. Therefore, the downside protection is theoretically only important in the near term. Mary wins in three out of four scenarios:

1. Win - Account remains static with no increase or decrease in value.
2. Win - Account increases in value.

---

[9] This hypothetical illustration assumes the drop in value occurs after the eligible period to recharacterize the Roth IRA conversion as described in Chapter Nine. It also assumes the same tax rate applies to both events.

3. Win - Account decreases in value but not below the taxable income threshold of $700,000 at the time of Roth conversion.

4. Lose – Account decreases below $700,000 at the time Mary needs to withdraw the funds.

It's interesting to note the "lose" scenario described above is not guaranteed to be a loss. For example, Mary only comes out behind if she has to withdraw the funds from the IRA when the account is below $700,000.[10] If she waits until the account rises above $700,000 based on future growth, she still wins even if the account value dips below $700,000 for some period of time.

Additionally, the "lose" scenario assumes tax rates are identical to when she did the Roth conversion. If tax rates increase over time as current law requires, the account could decrease even further before Mary loses on the Roth conversion. For example, assume her combined state and federal tax bracket at the time of withdrawal is fifty percent instead of forty percent as applied to the Roth conversion in the example. In that case, she still comes out ahead by having converted at the $700,000 level paying forty percent instead of withdrawing the same amount and paying fifty percent ($280,000 in tax versus $350,000 in tax).

---

[10] Also note that if Mary takes a full distribution of her Roth IRA and receives less than her basis in the account, she can recognize the loss as a miscellaneous itemized deduction. See IRA Publication 590 for more details on recognizing losses from IRA investments.

Chapter Eight

Too Good to Be True

Many things in life fall into the category of "too good to be true." These include calorie-free chocolate, a cell phone that never drops calls and dogs with minty-fresh breath. The huge tax savings described for Roth conversions and other IRA transactions throughout this book are thankfully both good and true.

In fact, some IRA owners have likely benefited from discounted asset valuations on their transactions without even knowing it thanks to the Financial Industry Regulatory Authority, Inc., or FINRA as it is commonly known. FINRA is the independent regulator for securities firms in the United States. They issue rules governing how securities firms operate, and work to ensure fair and honest dealings within the industry.

One rule enforced by FINRA relates to information reported on customer account statements. Specifically, it details how firms are to report per share values for illiquid securities known as direct participation programs (DPPs) and unlisted REITs.[1] A DPP is generally an investment vehicle which provides for flow through tax treatment of its activities regardless of the actual entity organization type such as LP or LLC.[2] Hedge funds, PIFs and other alternative investments are typically considered DPPs. DPPs/REITs are not listed on trading exchanges and are generally illiquid and difficult to value. The rule provides that brokerage firms may report estimated per share values derived from annual reports of the investment sponsor if available. Such

---

[1] NASD Rule 2340

[2] FINRA Rule 2310(a)(4)

estimated values must be no more than eighteen months old. If brokerage firms have reason to believe the value is inaccurate, they may refrain from reporting said value. Additionally, firms are authorized to obtain estimated per share values from an independent valuation source. Firms may also decline to report a value (except in certain circumstances) provided they make certain disclosures on the client account statement.

Consider the private REIT valuation policy of one large well known brokerage/custodial firm. This firm has a three step process to determine FMV for reporting purposes:

1. FMV provided by REIT sponsor annually.
2. Unrestricted active redemption program.
3. Independently reported secondary market transactions.

The brokerage firm first looks to the REIT sponsor for annually updated values. If these are not present or believed inaccurate by the firm, they look for any share buyback programs from the sponsor (redemption programs). Any such program must be unrestricted meaning an investor can liquidate any number of shares at any time (full liquidity). If there is no redemption program meeting the criteria, the firm seeks independent information regarding sales of the REIT shares on a secondary market. If none of these values are believed reasonable by the firm, they generally do not report an estimated per share value for the REIT on client account statements for that period.

A recent review of valuations reported by this firm reflects the following:

Table 6

REIT	Recent Statement Price	IRS Reporting Price (1099R, 5498, etc.)	Discount
REIT 1	$4.55	$2.57	-43%
REIT 2	$7.66	$3.14	-59%
REIT 3	$8.03	$6.02	-25%
REIT 4	$6.85	$4.93	-28%
REIT 5	$7.32	$5.70	-22%
Average Discount			**-35%**

In each case, the tax reporting value was derived from secondary market transactions while the most recent statement pricing was generally from sponsor reported information.

Imagine George decides to do a Roth conversion of a traditional IRA holding REIT 1 shares. George has a total value of $100,000 as reported on a recent account statement at the per share price of $4.55. He calculates the estimated tax on the conversion to be $40,000 based on this amount of reportable income.[3] However, when he receives Form 1099-R from the brokerage firm, it shows a taxable value of only $57,000. This reflects the forty-three percent discount the firm applied to the shares for tax reporting purposes. That's a nice surprise and saves George over $17,000! In fact, the tax owed comes to just $22,800 which is only twenty-two point eight percent (22.8%) of the last reported NAV of $100,000. Clearly "too good to be true" does not apply in this case.

---

[3] Assumes combined state and federal income tax bracket of 40%.

Also consider the range of discounts seen in closed end funds as referenced in Chapter Four. Custodial brokerage firms properly use the current FMV as determined from bid/ask trading prices on the exchange(s) when reporting on client IRA transactions and account statements. It would be a violation of both industry rules and the IRA reporting rules to show closed end fund shares at their NAV price which is almost always different than the trading price. In fact, most professional advisors would be outraged if one of their clients' Roth conversions was erroneously reported at NAV for a closed end fund trading at a large discount. They would fight tooth and nail to have the valuation corrected so their client only paid tax on the proper FMV. Imagine the similar outcry if the taxable capital gain on a sale of closed end fund shares was reported based on the higher NAV rather than the actual sale price (FMV).

In fact, it is more common for taxpayers and IRA custodians to report excess values thus incurring more tax than actually required. This is because the most common occurrence is for account statements and tax reporting documents from custodians to reflect the original cost basis in an asset. For example, the same brokerage firm reporting the discounts shown in Table Six currently reports sixteen other unlisted REITs at their original purchase price of $10. In some cases this value comes from the sponsor and in others there is no readily determinable FMV so they revert to cost basis as the proper reporting value. Either way, it is unlikely that every one of those sixteen REITs have a true FMV of $10 per share given the state of the real estate markets today. It is almost certain they are worth more or less than their original offering price.

The same is true of IRA custodians holding other alternative assets such as business interests, promissory notes, etc. Absent a formal appraisal, most custodians continue to report the asset at its original purchase price including on Form 1099-R and

Form 5498. This has caused untold additional and unnecessary amounts of tax to be paid on transactions involving these accounts including Roth conversions, distributions, RMD calculations, estate tax, gifting, etc.

The strategy of discount valuation as a tax mitigation tool is already being applied by custodians as evidenced by the list of discounted REITs on page sixty-three. This is simply by virtue of adhering to the rules of their industry and the IRA reporting regulations provided by the IRS. This fact should be comforting to anyone reading this book and thinking such tax savings are too good to be true. Some readers may now realize they paid tax on various transactions based on erroneous or inflated values. You should consult with your professional advisors to determine if such an error actually occurred and decide the best solution.

Chapter Nine

But I Already Did a Roth Conversion!

Many of you are wishing you'd read this book sooner and could go back in time to redo your Roth conversion(s) applying the information you've learned so far. You can... maybe.

Roth conversions are unique in that you can change your mind after the fact. The transaction is called a "recharacterization." The IRA owner recharacterizes their Roth conversion back into a traditional IRA, and it's as though the conversion transaction never occurred.[1] And since the conversion is deemed to have never occurred, there is no tax consequence to the IRA owner. No harm, no foul as they say.

However, there is a deadline for undoing Roth conversions. Recharacterizations are only allowed up until the IRA owner's tax filing deadline, including extensions, for the year of the Roth conversion.[2] That date is October 15th of the year following the year of the conversion. Consider a Roth conversion done in January 2011. The IRA owner will report the transaction on their 2011 tax return which is due by October 15th, 2012, at the latest. In that case, the IRA owner has effectively twenty-one and a half months (January 2011 until mid-October 2012) to review the transaction and change their mind. Let that sink in for a moment. It means that Roth conversions are completely risk-free transactions in the near term. There aren't too many deals like this in the tax code.

---

[1] IRC 408A(d)(6)

[2] IRC 408A(d)(7)

A person can convert to a Roth IRA without even considering whether it's a good idea because they have so much time to make the final decision. Even conversions done at the end of the year have at least nine and a half months to be reviewed before a final decision is required. This applies to Roth conversions done in December which must be reported by the following October 15th filing deadline.

Case Study – Lauren's 2011 Roth Conversion

Lauren converts her traditional IRA to a Roth IRA in April 2011. The IRA holds various stocks and some cash. The total account value at the time of conversion was $200,000, and she has sufficient non-IRA funds to pay the tax when she files her 2011 return by October 15th, 2012. The following factors would cause Lauren and her advisors to consider a recharacterization:

1. Account value drops: If the assets in the new Roth IRA decrease significantly in value, Lauren should consider undoing the conversion. For example, assume the account is worth only $150,000 by the time she's ready to file her return. Lauren should recharacterize, otherwise, she will be reporting $200,000 of income and paying the associated tax for an asset that is only worth $150,000.

2. Tax rates decrease: OK, I agree this one is highly unlikely, but it should be included. If the government were to enact reduced tax rates that became effective in 2012 or 2013, Lauren should consider a recharacterization. This would avoid her paying tax on the conversion at the higher 2011 rates in our hypothetical scenario. She could later reconvert (we'll explain that shortly) and lock in the new lower tax rates.

3. Lower tax bracket: This refers to Lauren's personal tax

situation for the year in question. For example, Lauren may have had a very high income year in 2011 and is expected to be in a much lower tax bracket in 2012 or 2013. In that scenario, she may want to recharacterize her Roth conversion and wait to reconvert in the appropriate year to take advantage of the lower tax bracket.

4. <u>Lauren didn't use a discount valuation strategy:</u> Unfortunately for Lauren and her advisors, this book wasn't available in April 2011 (gasp!). So they didn't know about some of the opportunities available to reduce the taxable value of her Roth conversion. This might also be a good reason to consider a recharacterization before the filing deadline. She can then start over by applying the discounting strategy and reconverting later.

The other great thing about the Roth conversion rules (besides being able to change your mind after the conversion) is that you can reconvert again later. It's not a one shot deal. If an IRA owner converts, then later decides to recharacterize the conversion, they can still do another Roth conversion with the same assets at a later time. The rule is that after recharacterizing, you must wait until:

> "…the taxable year following the taxable year in which the amount was converted to a Roth IRA or, if later, the end of the 30-day period beginning on the day on which the IRA owner transfers the amount from the Roth IRA back to a traditional IRA by means of a recharacterization…"[3]

Using Lauren's case study, if she recharacterizes anytime in 2012, she must wait thirty days to reconvert. Thirty days is the later date because 2012 is already the next tax year following her

---

[3] Treasury Regulations Section 1.408A-5, A-9

original year of Roth conversion (2011). If she recharacterizes on November 10th, 2011 (the same year she did the original Roth conversion) she must wait until January 1st, 2012, which is the next tax year and is longer than thirty days from the date of recharacterization.

If you recently completed a Roth conversion and are still within the timeline to recharacterize, you have the opportunity to go back, undo the conversion and apply a discount valuation strategy before reconverting, if appropriate. Professional advisors should also review client transactions to see if recharacterizing makes sense in light of the tax saving opportunities outlined in this book.

Chapter Ten

Asset Class Segregation

This strategy is not specific to IRAs utilizing discounted assets but should be considered in conjunction with any large Roth conversion.

Asset class segregation involves separating the traditional IRA into different accounts based on asset classes prior to doing Roth conversions on each. This allows the IRA owner and their advisors to consider each asset separately for possible recharacterization prior to the tax filing deadline described in Chapter Nine.

Case Study –
Hunter's IRA Owns Multiple Asset Classes

Hunter's IRA holds the following assets:

Mutual fund A (US large cap growth)	$100,000
Mutual fund B (Emerging markets)	$100,000
Mutual fund C (Government bond fund)	$100,000
Total IRA Value	**$300,000**

Hunter's advisors recommend a Roth conversion in May 2011. They also wisely suggest that he separate the IRA into three new IRAs each holding one particular mutual fund. Once the accounts are segregated by asset class Hunter converts each into a separate Roth IRA. He and his advisors have until October 15th, 2012, to watch each asset and make final determinations on whether to let the Roth conversions stand or do recharacterizations. The advantage is they can choose to recharacterize just one and not necessarily all three. Hunter and his advisors review the Roth IRAs in September 2012. Here are the updated account values:

Roth IRA A – mutual fund A	$130,000
Roth IRA B – mutual fund B	$120,000
Roth IRA C – mutual fund C	$50,000
Total Roth IRA Value	**$300,000**

Roth IRAs A and B have increased nicely while Roth IRA C has lost fifty percent of its pre-conversion value. Overall, the total value is still $300,000. If the assets had not been segregated, it would look as though not much had happened. The traditional IRA was $300,000 at the time of conversion and the total value is still $300,000. In that case, Hunter would likely be advised to let the Roth conversion stand and go ahead and pay the associated tax.

Instead, Hunter has additional options because the assets were segregated into different IRAs. He will keep Roth IRAs A and B since he will only pay tax on the combined conversion amount of $200,000 and the accounts are worth $250,000 currently. Roth IRA C will be recharacterized back into a traditional IRA because it doesn't make sense to pay tax on the original conversion value of $100,000 for an asset that is only worth $50,000 now. After recharacterizing, Hunter can wait the required time and then reconvert the account back into a Roth IRA. The tax owed on the new Roth conversion will be based on the current value of $50,000 (assuming no change in value between recharacterization and reconversion dates).

It is important to note that Hunter must segregate the asset classes via multiple IRAs in order to maintain the option of recharacterizing only the losing asset. The rules do allow for a partial recharacterization, but they do not allow an IRA owner to pick and choose which assets and values to recharacterize out of one large Roth IRA.[1]

---

[1] Treasury Regulations Section 1.408A-5, A-2(c)(5), (c)(6) Example 2

Chapter Eleven

Tax Alchemy: Converting Ordinary Income to Capital Gains

It sounds funny, but under the tax rules, this type of turning lead into gold actually works. Distributions from traditional IRAs are taxed as ordinary income in the year received.[1] This includes capital gains that may have built up in the account over time. Every dollar is taxed as ordinary income regardless of what its tax nature would be outside the IRA. Thus basis and capital gains are treated the same. The IRA owner is not allowed to separate capital gains from basis attributable to deductible IRA contributions and apply capital gains tax rates to the former and ordinary income rates to the latter. This creates an opportunity when making "in kind" distributions of discounted assets.

An in kind distribution occurs when the IRA owner has the custodian distribute shares or fractional interests of the actual underlying IRA investments. For example, an IRA holding 1000 shares of XYZ stock distributes 200 shares of the stock. The same can be done with shares of a mutual fund, REIT, closed end fund or any asset provided it can be divided into separate parts/shares/percentages/etc. Individual bonds and certificates of deposit (CDs) can also be distributed in kind from an IRA to the owner.

In each case, the FMV of the asset on the date of distribution is reported on the Form 1099-R as taxable income in the year of the distribution. So if XYZ shares were valued at $50 per

---

[1] IRC 408(d) & Treasury Regulations Section 1.408-4(a)(1)

share on the date of distribution, the taxable income to the IRA owner would be $10,000 (200 shares x $50/share). Note the entire FMV of the assets at distribution is reported and taxed as ordinary income regardless of whether a majority of the value in the shares was from capital gain.

Assume an IRA purchases XYZ stock for $10 per share. XYZ rises to $50 per share over a period of three years. The IRA owner withdraws 200 shares of XYZ from the IRA which have a basis of $2000 (200 shares x $10/share purchase price) and current FMV of $10,000 (200 shares x $50/share current price). The IRA owner reports the full $10,000 as ordinary income and gets a "step up" in basis such that $10,000 is now his basis outside the IRA when determining any future capital gains or losses.[2] At a combined state and federal income tax bracket of forty percent, the tax owed is $4000.

If the same shares had been purchased with non-IRA funds at $10/share and subsequently sold at $50/share, the tax result would have been vastly different. Only the gain would have been taxable and then at the long-term capital gains rate, currently fifteen percent. The total tax would have been $1200 ($8000 capital gain x 15% CG tax). Obviously, this comparison is not apples to apples since we have not considered the potential advantage of the IRA in the form of an upfront tax deduction at the time of contribution(s) and year to year tax protection on overall investment activity inside the account.

---

[2] Treasury Regulations Section 1.408A-6, A-16 specifically refers to FMV as the basis of assets distributed in kind from Roth IRAs. Section 1.408-4(a)(2) states that a person's basis in a traditional IRA is zero when determining tax treatment of distributions. Paying tax on the distributed value creates a new basis at the distributed FMV for purposes of determining tax on future dispositions of the asset(s).

However, it does highlight the significant variation in tax impact between ordinary income and capital gains. The question becomes: How can one obtain the more favorable capital gains tax treatment on ordinary income IRA distributions? Answer: Make in kind distributions of assets subject to discounted valuation adjustments.

Case Study – Traditional IRA Distributing Private Investment Fund (PIF) Shares

Jack's traditional IRA holds an interest in a private investment fund (PIF). The NAV of Jack's interest is $1,000,000. A qualified appraisal reports the FMV to be $700,000, a thirty percent discount from NAV. For simplicity, we will assume Jack distributes the entire asset at once. This causes a Form 1099-R to be issued reporting $700,000 of taxable income. Remember the reported and recognized income is based on the FMV of the distribution, not the NAV.

The PIF interest is now held by Jack personally with a cost basis of $700,000. Thus any future capital gains or losses are based on this figure. Assume the PIF liquidates more than twelve months later with no additional growth, and Jack receives his full $1,000,000 NAV. The $300,000 difference between his cost basis ($700,000) and the amount received at the liquidation of the PIF ($1,000,000) is long-term capital gain. At today's long-term capital gains tax rate of fifteen percent, Jack owes $45,000 in capital gains tax. He would have owed $120,000 if the $300,000 had been taxed as ordinary income at the time of distribution from the IRA.[3]

Jack saved $75,000 in tax by converting $300,000 of ordinary income into capital gain. He also deferred payment of the tax

---

[3] Assumes combined state and federal income tax bracket of 40%.

until the PIF liquidated one year after the IRA distribution. This
allowed Jack to continue earning interest in the meantime on the
money used to pay the tax.

Here is a side by side comparison of the tax effect of
distributing assets at full NAV versus distributing discounted
assets and obtaining capital gains treatment on the discounted
portion:

Table 7

	Distribution at Full NAV	Distribution w/ Reduced FMV
IRA NAV	$1,000,000	$1,000,000
Valuation Adjustment	N/A	30%
IRA FMV	$1,000,000	$700,000
OI[4] Tax on Distribution	($400,000)	($280,000)
LTCG Tax[5] on $300k discount	N/A	($45,000)
Total Tax	($400,000)	($325,000)
Net Tax Advantage	--	**+$75,000**

Note that if the asset is liquidated less than twelve months
from the date of in kind distribution from the traditional IRA,
any gain above FMV at the time of distribution will be taxed as
short-term capital gains. Short-term capital gains are taxed at

---

[4] Ordinary income tax.

[5] Long-term capital gains tax at 15%.

the same rates as ordinary income, so no tax savings results in this scenario. To achieve the savings offered from converting ordinary income into capital gains, the asset must qualify for long-term capital gain treatment. This means holding the distributed asset more than twelve months before an event causing recognition of the gain (sale or liquidation).

Additionally, both the case study and Table Seven assume no change in value of the distributed asset between the date of distribution and the event causing recognition of capital gain. In the case study, the recognition event was the liquidation of the PIF which is deemed to be a sale transaction and thus triggers the recognition of capital gain if applicable. If the asset increases in value post-IRA distribution, the additional value will be recognized as capital gain as well. Conversely, if the asset decreases in value, but is still worth more than the FMV on the date of withdrawal from the IRA, the taxable capital gain will be less. And if the value of the asset drops below the FMV from the time of withdrawal from the IRA, a capital loss may result.

Chapter Twelve

Reducing Required Minimum Distributions

As we've seen, distributions from traditional IRAs are generally subject to ordinary income tax in the year of withdrawal. Traditional IRA owners must also comply with mandatory minimum distribution rules that kick in once the IRA owner turns age 70 ½.[1] These are called required minimum distributions (RMDs).[2]

In a nutshell, it's like the government saying: "Ok, the free ride is over. We've waited this long to tax this account, we're not waiting any longer. Start pulling the money out now...or else!"[3] The amount required to be withdrawn each year is based on life expectancy tables provided by the IRS. The general approach or theory is that the account will be essentially totally withdrawn over the course of the IRA owner's expected lifetime. It is irrelevant that this doesn't generally happen. The important point is traditional IRA owners must begin withdrawing funds and reporting the income for tax purposes.

---

[1] IRC 408(a)(6) & 408(b)(3)

[2] Sometimes also referred to as minimum required distributions (MRDs).

[3] IRC 4974 imposes an excise tax of 50% of any amount required to be distributed but which remains in the IRA.

The basic process for determining how much is required to be withdrawn is:

1. Determine the FMV of the traditional IRA as of December 31st.
2. Review the applicable life expectancy table provided by the IRS (Table I, Table II or Table III) and find the appropriate factor.[4]
3. Divide the value from step 1 by the factor in step 2.
4. The result is the RMD for the current tax year (the year following the December 31st valuation date).

Distributions to satisfy RMD requirements also trigger a Form 1099-R from the IRA custodian. Just as in the Roth conversion scenarios previously outlined, the custodian is required to report the FMV of the distribution.

The amount of distribution each year is partially dependent on the FMV of the IRA. A large FMV results in a larger required distribution. A reduced FMV results in a lower required distribution. Here is an example of how a valuation discount can result in a significantly reduced RMD for a seventy-five year old IRA owner:

---

[4] Table I is for use by beneficiaries of inherited IRAs. Table II is for IRA owners with a spouse more than 10 years younger as the sole IRA beneficiary. Table III is for unmarried IRA owners, owners with spouses less than 10 years younger and owners whose spouses are not the sole beneficiary. All three tables may be found in Appendices A, B and C, respectively.

Table 8

	RMD at Full NAV	RMD w/ Discounted FMV
IRA NAV	$1,000,000	$1,000,000
Valuation Adjustment	N/A	30%
IRA FMV	$1,000,000	$700,000
Life Expectancy Factor[5]	22.9	22.9
RMD[6]	$43,700	$30,600

The owner of the IRA without a discount valuation strategy is required to take an extra $13,100 from their IRA. *That's an extra $13,100 of taxable income!* This same scenario will repeat each year wherein the full NAV account will be forced to make a larger taxable distribution than the discounted account assuming similar NAV on both.

[5] Using Table III (Uniform Life Table) value for a 75 year old IRA owner. See Appendix C.

[6] Rounded to nearest $100.

The Super Stretch IRA

The term "stretch IRA" is not a technical term found in the tax code. It is rather a term of art used in the tax planning community to describe an IRA that is subject to RMDs "stretched" out over the life of an IRA beneficiary.

Beneficiary IRA or inherited IRA are the terms used to denote an IRA that has been inherited by a beneficiary following the death of the original IRA owner. The rules about handling distributions from a beneficiary IRA become rather complex with multiple variables depending on how old the IRA owner was at death, who the beneficiaries are, the age of the beneficiaries and more. These rules are beyond the scope of this section and are not reviewed in detail here.[1]

For this section we will assume the following:

- Beneficiary is not the IRA owner's spouse
- Beneficiary is not a charity, the estate or other entity without a measurable lifespan
- Beneficiary is a living individual
- IRA owner died prior to age 70 ½

When the above criteria are present, the beneficiary is required to take RMDs from the IRA based on their own life expectancy. They have the option to pull money out of the inherited IRA any time and in any amount desired, subject to ordinary income tax

---

[1] For further information on this topic, see IRS Publication 590 available at www. irs.gov.

just as any other traditional IRA distribution. There are no age related penalties associated with such withdrawals even if the beneficiary receiving the distributions is under age 59 ½. This is because the death of the original IRA owner falls under one of the exceptions to the early withdrawal penalty.[2]

This provides an opportunity for younger generation beneficiaries to stretch required withdrawals over their own life expectancy maintaining the tax advantages of the IRA potentially for decades.

Case Study – Value of Stretch IRA over 30 Years

Robert dies in 2011 at age sixty-one with a traditional IRA valued at $1,000,000. His son, Bob Jr., is the sole beneficiary of the IRA. Bob Jr. is thirty years old at the time of his father's death. If Bob Jr. takes only the RMD each year for the next thirty years, his inherited IRA will grow to $4,420,000 by the time Bob Jr. is age sixty.[3] He will also have received $2,245,000 in cumulative distributions during that time. Those are amazing results and truly reflect the power of using the stretch option for beneficiary IRAs. Table Nine shows the annual RMDs to Bob Jr. and year end values over the next thirty years:[4]

---

[2] IRC Section 72

[3] Assumes hypothetical annual rate of return of 8% .

[4] All dollar amounts shown in thousands.

Table 9

As of 31-Dec	Age Year End	Previous Year End NAV	Life Expectancy	RMD
2012	31	$1,000.00	52.4	$19.08
2013	32	$1,060.92	51.4	$20.64
2014	33	$1,125.15	50.4	$22.32
2015	34	$1,192.84	49.4	$24.15
2016	35	$1,264.12	48.4	$26.12
2017	36	$1,339.13	47.4	$28.25
2018	37	$1,418.01	46.4	$30.56
2019	38	$1,500.89	45.4	$33.06
2020	39	$1,587.90	44.4	$35.76
2021	40	$1,679.17	43.4	$38.69
2022	41	$1,774.81	42.4	$41.86
2023	42	$1,874.94	41.4	$45.29
2024	43	$1,979.64	40.4	$49.00
2025	44	$2,089.01	39.4	$53.02
2026	45	$2,203.11	38.4	$57.37
2027	46	$2,321.99	37.4	$62.09
2028	47	$2,445.66	36.4	$67.19
2029	48	$2,574.13	35.4	$72.72
2030	49	$2,707.34	34.4	$78.70
2031	50	$2,845.23	33.4	$85.19
2032	51	$2,987.66	32.4	$92.21
2033	52	$3,134.46	31.4	$99.82
2034	53	$3,285.39	30.4	$108.07
2035	54	$3,440.15	29.4	$117.01
2036	55	$3,598.35	28.4	$126.70
2037	56	$3,759.52	27.4	$137.21
2038	57	$3,923.07	26.4	$148.60
2039	58	$4,088.32	25.4	$160.96
2040	59	$4,254.43	24.4	$174.36
2041	60	$4,420.42	23.4	$188.91

Now let's apply the Super Stretch IRA strategy to the same set of facts. Remember from Chapter Twelve, RMDs are partly based on the IRA value as of December 31st each year. When an IRA owns an asset subject to valuation adjustments, the discounted FMV as of December 31st serves to reduce the RMD in the following year. Assume the IRA owns shares of a PIF subject to discount valuation adjustments. The result is that Bob Jr. doesn't have to take as much out of the inherited IRA each year which leaves more money in the account to compound tax protected over time.

Using a $1,000,000 NAV with a thirty percent adjustment to $700,000 FMV in the first year, here are the results:[5]

---

[5] Assumes hypothetical constant 30% valuation discount from NAV for all years. All dollar amounts shown in thousands.

Table 10

As of 31-Dec	Age Year End	Previous Year End NAV	Previous Year End FMV	Life Expectancy	RMD
2012	31	$1,000.00	$700.00	52.4	$13.36
2013	32	$1,066.64	$746.65	51.4	$14.53
2014	33	$1,137.45	$796.21	50.4	$15.80
2015	34	$1,212.64	$848.85	49.4	$17.18
2016	35	$1,292.47	$904.73	48.4	$18.69
2017	36	$1,377.18	$964.02	47.4	$20.34
2018	37	$1,467.01	$1,026.91	46.4	$22.13
2019	38	$1,562.24	$1,093.57	45.4	$24.09
2020	39	$1,663.13	$1,164.19	44.4	$26.22
2021	40	$1,769.97	$1,238.98	43.4	$28.55
2022	41	$1,883.01	$1,318.11	42.4	$31.09
2023	42	$2,002.57	$1,401.80	41.4	$33.86
2024	43	$2,128.91	$1,490.24	40.4	$36.89
2025	44	$2,262.34	$1,583.64	39.4	$40.19
2026	45	$2,403.13	$1,682.19	38.4	$43.81
2027	46	$2,551.58	$1,786.10	37.4	$47.76
2028	47	$2,707.95	$1,895.56	36.4	$52.08
2029	48	$2,872.51	$2,010.75	35.4	$56.80
2030	49	$3,045.51	$2,131.85	34.4	$61.97
2031	50	$3,227.17	$2,259.02	33.4	$67.64
2032	51	$3,417.71	$2,392.40	32.4	$73.84
2033	52	$3,617.29	$2,532.10	31.4	$80.64
2034	53	$3,826.03	$2,678.22	30.4	$88.10
2035	54	$4,044.02	$2,830.81	29.4	$96.29
2036	55	$4,271.25	$2,989.88	28.4	$105.28
2037	56	$4,507.67	$3,155.37	27.4	$115.16
2038	57	$4,753.13	$3,327.19	26.4	$126.03
2039	58	$5,007.35	$3,505.14	25.4	$138.00
2040	59	$5,269.94	$3,688.96	24.4	$151.19
2041	60	$5,540.35	$3,878.24	23.4	$165.74

The cumulative income distributions to Bob Jr. are $1,813,000, and the NAV of the account at the end of thirty years is $5,540,000. That's a $1,120,000 increase in the size of the tax protected IRA versus the regular stretch IRA option. Clearly, applying valuation adjustment principles can provide meaningful positive impacts on the long-term value of inherited IRAs.

Chapter Fourteen

The Lifetime Stretch IRA

As described earlier, the concept of a stretch IRA is used to describe an inherited IRA subject to RMDs. The RMDs are "stretched" over the life expectancy of the beneficiary who is often much younger than the original IRA owner. This allows for many additional years of tax protected growth within the account.

RMDs that begin due to the IRA owner reaching age 70½ often serve to erode the value of the account over time. Technically, that is their intended purpose by forcing the owner to take taxable withdrawals from the account every year for the rest of their lives. In many cases, IRA owners do not want or need to take withdrawals from their traditional IRAs to meet personal living expenses. They often prefer to keep as much value in the tax protected account as possible and pass the additional value on to heirs or charity.

Luckily, we can apply the same stretch IRA principles seen in the last section effectively reducing the amount of the RMD and creating a stretch IRA scenario during the original account owner's life.

Case Study – Grace Maximizes IRA Bequest to Charity

Grace has substantial assets and will have an estate tax issue upon her passing. Part of her planning includes naming her church as the sole beneficiary of her sizeable traditional IRA. This provides two tax benefits:

1. Grace's estate will get a charitable estate tax deduction equal to the value of her IRA at the time of death.

2. As a tax exempt organization, the church will not incur income tax on the IRA assets when it withdraws funds from the account.

Naturally, Grace would like to leave the most value possible to her church which benefits the organization AND her estate. Grace recently reached age 70 ½ and must begin taking RMDs. She can reduce her RMDs as shown in Chapter Twelve by holding assets subject to valuation adjustment. This allows more funds to remain in the IRA and grow tax protected over Grace's lifetime.

The table on the next page shows the projected account value at the end of each year through Grace's age 90 using the following assumptions:

- Life expectancy numbers from Table III – Uniform Lifetime Table
- 6% annual rate of return
- No discount valuation strategy applied
- $1,000,000 original traditional IRA value
- No withdrawals other than applicable RMDs

As the data shows, at an annual return rate of six percent, the RMDs essentially stunt the growth of the IRA. After twenty years, the account has only grown to $1,075,800. That's only seven point five eight percent (7.58%) cumulative return over twenty years which equals zero point zero zero three seven percent (0.0037%) annualized!

Grace's goal to grow the value of the gift to charity was stymied by the taxable withdrawals she was forced to take each year.

Table 11

As of 31-Dec	Age Year End	Previous Year End Cash Value	Life Expectancy	RMD
2011	71	$1,000,000.00	26.5	$37,735.85
2012	72	$1,022,264.15	25.6	$39,932.19
2013	73	$1,043,667.81	24.7	$42,253.76
2014	74	$1,064,034.12	23.8	$44,707.32
2015	75	$1,083,168.85	22.9	$47,299.95
2016	76	$1,100,859.03	22	$50,039.05
2017	77	$1,116,871.52	21.2	$52,682.62
2018	78	$1,131,201.19	20.3	$55,724.20
2019	79	$1,143,349.06	19.5	$58,633.29
2020	80	$1,153,316.71	18.7	$61,674.69
2021	81	$1,160,841.02	17.9	$64,851.46
2022	82	$1,165,640.02	17.1	$68,166.08
2023	83	$1,167,412.34	16.3	$71,620.39
2024	84	$1,165,836.69	15.5	$75,215.27
2025	85	$1,160,571.62	14.8	$78,417.00
2026	86	$1,151,788.92	14.1	$81,687.16
2027	87	$1,139,209.10	13.4	$85,015.61
2028	88	$1,122,546.04	12.7	$88,389.45
2029	89	$1,101,509.35	12	$91,792.45
2030	90	$1,075,807.46	11.4	$94,369.08

What if Grace's IRA held assets subject to valuation adjustment that served to reduce her RMD over that same time period? Table Twelve shows the result of an asset discounted thirty percent held in the IRA during the same time frame.[1]

---

[1] Assumes hypothetical constant 30% valuation discount from NAV for all years.

Table 12

31-Dec	Age	Previous Year End NAV	Previous Year End FMV	Life Expectancy	RMD
2011	71	$1,000,000.00	$700,000.00	26.5	$26,415.09
2012	72	$1,033,584.91	$723,509.43	25.6	$28,262.09
2013	73	$1,067,337.91	$747,136.54	24.7	$30,248.44
2014	74	$1,101,129.74	$770,790.82	23.8	$32,386.17
2015	75	$1,134,811.36	$794,367.95	22.9	$34,688.56
2016	76	$1,168,211.49	$817,748.04	22	$37,170.37
2017	77	$1,201,133.81	$840,793.67	21.2	$39,660.08
2018	78	$1,233,541.76	$863,479.23	20.3	$42,535.92
2019	79	$1,265,018.34	$885,512.84	19.5	$45,410.91
2020	80	$1,295,508.53	$906,855.97	18.7	$48,494.97
2021	81	$1,324,744.07	$927,320.85	17.9	$51,805.63
2022	82	$1,352,423.08	$946,696.15	17.1	$55,362.35
2023	83	$1,378,206.11	$964,744.28	16.3	$59,186.77
2024	84	$1,401,711.71	$981,198.20	15.5	$63,303.11
2025	85	$1,422,511.31	$995,757.92	14.8	$67,280.94
2026	86	$1,440,581.05	$1,008,406.73	14.1	$71,518.21
2027	87	$1,455,497.70	$1,018,848.39	13.4	$76,033.46
2028	88	$1,466,794.10	$1,026,755.87	12.7	$80,846.92
2029	89	$1,473,954.83	$1,031,768.38	12	$85,980.70
2030	90	$1,476,411.42	$1,033,487.99	11.4	$90,656.84

The net advantage is over $400,000! The discounted IRA has more than $400,000 additional NAV after twenty years than the non-discounted IRA. This is a cumulative return of forty-seven point six percent (47.6%) which equals almost two percent annualized.

In order to realize the full benefit of the charitable gift deduction, the IRA will need to be valued at full NAV at the time of the gift to the church. Grace and her advisors will need to plan ahead to ensure the assets are converted to cash or otherwise not subject to discounting at that time. For example, many non-traded assets have automatic liquidation or cash out provisions which are triggered by the death of the owner.

The additional $400,000 of value gifted to Grace's church also provides an extra $140,000 of estate tax savings at today's maximum federal estate tax rate of thirty-five percent. It also significantly increases the philanthropic impact of her gift. Interestingly, the church may even have an interest in ensuring proper valuations are applied in order to protect their future interest in the account.

Chapter Fifteen

Reducing the Estate Tax Bite on IRAs

IRA assets are included in the value of the gross estate for estate tax calculations of a deceased person. This can have a devastating effect on the future value of the IRA. The top federal estate tax rate is currently thirty-five percent and scheduled to increase to fifty-five percent in less than two years. More than a third of the value of the IRA can be lost to estate tax at today's rate. And this calculation does not even consider the additional erosion effect caused by state inheritance or estate taxes depending on location.

The estate tax applies equally to traditional and Roth IRAs. So while Roth IRAs escape income tax on withdrawals under the right circumstances, they do not avoid the estate tax. This can cause a huge loss of future tax-free income potential in cases where Roth IRA assets are needed to pay the estate tax bill.

Discounted assets held in the IRA at death serve to reduce the value of the IRA when calculating the gross estate. This can provide very large estate tax savings as shown below:

Table 13

	IRA at Full NAV	IRA w/ Discounted FMV
IRA NAV	$1,000,000	$1,000,000
Valuation adjustment	N/A	30%
IRA FMV	$1,000,000	$700,000
Estate tax (35%)	($350,000)	($245,000)
Net Tax Advantage		**+$105,000**

The IRA on the left would need to make an extra ten point five percent (10.5%) investment gain to make up for the tax savings achieved in the IRA on the right. This percentage is based on the NAV before estate tax of $1,000,000. If the dollars to pay the estate tax came out of the IRA, the percentage required would be much higher. Most people would be happy to earn an extra ten point five percent (10.5%) return via tax savings on their IRAs.

In addition to estate tax, beneficiaries must pay income tax on withdrawals from an inherited traditional IRA creating a huge double hit to the account value. There is one small consolation in the law for such cases. The beneficiary is entitled to an income tax deduction equal to the amount of estate tax paid as a result of the IRA value. This is often referred to as a Section 691(c) deduction referring to the section of tax code where it is found.

Here is an example of how significant the combination of estate tax followed by income tax can be on a traditional IRA, even taking into account the Section 691(c) deduction:

Traditional IRA	$ 1,000,000
Estate tax[1]	$ (350,000)
Income tax[2]	$ (260,000)
Net to beneficiary[3]	**$ 390,000**

---

[1] Assumes maximum current federal estate tax rate of 35%.

[2] Assumes combined state and federal income tax bracket of 40% and takes into account the Section 691(c) deduction allowed for the estate tax paid above.

[3] A very unhappy beneficiary!

Now consider the same scenario (estate tax preceding income tax) except the IRA holds an asset discounted by thirty percent:

Traditional IRA NAV	$ 1,000,000
Traditional IRA FMV	$ 700,000
Estate tax	$ (245,000)
Income tax[4]	$ (182,000)
Net to beneficiary[5]	**$ 573,000**

Applying the same tax rates to a traditional IRA discounted by thirty percent, results in $573,000 net to the beneficiary compared with only $390,000 in the previous scenario. This provides an increase of $183,000 transferred within the family rather than lost to tax erosion.

---

[4] Assumes assets distributed in kind with $700,000 FMV as taxable income and applies the Section 691(c) deduction allowed for the estate tax paid above.

[5] Reflects full NAV minus estate and income tax paid.

Chapter Sixteen

Risks

Intelligent reasonable people can have different opinions on how to estimate FMV of illiquid assets. In some cases involving valuation adjustments, the IRS tries to argue for a lower discount such as fifteen percent instead of thirty percent. In other cases, particularly charitable gift deductions, the IRS often argues for higher discounts such as fifty percent instead of twenty-five percent. If successful, these arguments can reduce the ultimate tax benefit for the taxpayer. It is very common for the IRS to argue both sides of the valuation issue depending on which viewpoint best serves their interest of raising maximum tax revenue in a particular case.

This creates an inherent risk to IRA owners when using assets subject to valuation adjustments in their taxable IRA transactions. Specifically, the IRS may conduct an audit and decide to challenge the valuation applied to the asset(s). It is important to note that when done properly, the amount of valuation adjustment is the only reasonable argument by the IRS in these scenarios. They and the tax court have been very explicit that FMV is the proper valuation when reporting IRA transactions. They and the tax court have been similarly explicit in defining how to determine FMV of non-traded assets. Therefore, the only subjective issue to be challenged is the correct FMV.

That is why this book and reputable advisors constantly highlight the use of qualified appraisers to determine accurate

FMV of non-traded assets.[1] If a reported FMV is successfully challenged by the IRS and the final FMV is adjusted upward, the IRA owner will generally be liable for any additional taxes owed on their transaction(s). They may also be liable for other penalties and interest depending on the specific circumstances. Engaging a truly qualified professional to perform necessary appraisal work will substantially mitigate the risk of an incorrect valuation.

For example, assume an unqualified person determines an IRA asset has a NAV of $100,000 and FMV of $70,000 (thirty percent adjustment). The IRA owner does a Roth conversion and pays tax based on the unreliable FMV. The IRS successfully challenges the valuation such that the final FMV is determined to be $90,000. In this scenario, the taxpayer will owe additional tax on the conversion for the extra $20,000 of income. They may also be liable for other penalties and interest depending on a variety of factors.

There have been cases where unscrupulous advisors have concocted various schemes and transactions that have been rightfully challenged and shot down in tax court. One particular type of IRA transaction became so prevalent that the IRS issued a formal notice as a warning to taxpayers.[2] The transactions in the notice involved taxpayers with an existing business that would set up a Roth IRA owned "shell" company. The taxpayer's existing business would then engage in various sham transactions with the Roth owned company such that the Roth

[1] The law does not specifically require a qualified appraiser as defined in IRC 170(f)(11)(E)(i). Meeting this standard exceeds current requirements and industry practices. See also: Internal Revenue Manual section 4.72.8.1.2 – "…there is no absolute requirement the annual valuation be based on an independent appraisal."; Treasury Regulations Section 1.408A-7, A-2

[2] Notice 2004-8

owned company ended up miraculously holding significant assets. These transactions avoided the Roth IRA contribution limits and caused substantial non-IRA assets to be fraudulently transferred into the Roth IRA. The notice declares these and similar transactions to be "listed transactions" which means they must be reported to the IRS by the taxpayer among other requirements.

Another version that has come to light recently involved traditional IRA owners doing a similar transaction between a shell company owned by their traditional IRA and another shell company owned by their Roth IRA. The end result was determined to be the same in that excess monies flowed from the traditional IRA to the Roth IRA in violation of the contribution limits.

One common factor in these scam artist scenarios is they cannot cite proper references or guidance for the positions or transactions they propose. It usually boils down to convincing the client they know what they're doing and the client just trusts that they do. This should be a red flag to a reasonable person. A key takeaway from these case studies is to get independent review and advice prior to engaging in any transaction that may impact your tax situation.

There is an old saying that "pigs get fat but hogs get slaughtered." There is no need to engage in shady transactions in attempts to skirt the law to gain tax benefits. It also isn't necessary to try to stretch or game valuation adjustments to get better numbers. Substantial legitimate tax advantages are available from even modest discounts. And as reviewed earlier, there are many common investment assets that you or your clients may already own which are candidates for valuation adjustments. Bottom line to reduce risk: seek qualified professional advice, use reputable qualified appraisers, follow the rules religiously and great tax results will follow.

PART THREE

Leveraged IRA Transactions

Chapter Seventeen

The Leveraged IRA

(WARNING: The use of leverage causes additional risk to the IRA and is not appropriate for everyone. In some cases, leverage can add the risk of losing the entire IRA. The following chapters are NOT a recommendation to utilize debt within an IRA. They are only intended to review the tax ramifications of various IRA transactions when debt is involved. IRA owners should consult with their professional advisors and carefully consider the potential advantages and disadvantages before using leverage within their IRA.)

Most people view the total value of their IRA as the maximum amount available to invest. However, IRAs are eligible to borrow money for investment purposes just like individuals, businesses and trusts. This allows IRAs to put the age old concept of using "other people's money" to work in hopes of earning a return greater than the loan costs such as interest, points, etc. As we'll review in the next few chapters, this can also create substantial tax saving opportunities on IRA transactions.

As with any IRA related transaction, there are some strict rules to be aware of and follow for the loan to qualify. The following sections review some important considerations when using leverage inside an IRA.

Nonrecourse Loans

The first rule to be aware of is that any loans to an IRA must be nonrecourse. A nonrecourse loan is one where the lender's only remedy in the event of default by the borrower is to foreclose on any property or assets used as collateral to secure the loan. The lender cannot retain the right to go after additional assets held by the IRA or IRA owner personally.

IRA owners and disqualified persons are prohibited from personally guaranteeing debt of an IRA. To understand this better, imagine a scenario where an IRA borrows money for a real estate purchase that goes sour. The IRA defaults on the loan with no cash available to continue making loan payments. If the IRA owner had personally guaranteed the loan, he would be expected to cover the loan payments directly to the lender out of personal funds. The net result would be the avoidance of foreclosure by the IRA. The IRA would be able to keep the property and continue to profit from any future rental income or capital appreciation. This would add significant value to the IRA and prevent the loss of the asset used as collateral.

Such a scenario violates the prohibited transaction rules and disqualifies the account as an IRA. Any "extension of credit" between the IRA and its owner is a prohibited transaction (PT).[1] So the mere act of guaranteeing the debt caused a PT at the time of the original loan. The ramification of this is that the IRA is no longer an IRA.[2] All assets are deemed distributed and subject to tax and potentially penalties.[3]

What if the owner made the loan payments on behalf of the IRA but had not personally guaranteed the debt at the time of the loan? This is also a problem and violates another rule. IRAs are considered to be trusts and have designated trustees

---

[1] IRC 4975(c)(1)(B)

[2] IRC 408(e)(2)(A)

[3] IRC 408(e)(2)(B

which are typically either banks or other approved custodians.[4] All contributions to IRAs must be made in cash.[5] Contributions must go through the trustee/custodian who is responsible for holding and reporting on the IRA assets. Therefore, direct loan payments from the IRA owner to the lender would be considered improper contributions to the IRA.

Here is an easy way to understand this principle: Heather opens an IRA at her local bank and makes a small initial deposit of $100. She then goes home and sticks a label to an old coffee can that reads "Heather's IRA." She "deposits" $500 cash into the coffee can and puts it in the cupboard. Does Heather now have an IRA worth $600? No! The funds may have been in cash per the rule, but they weren't given to the trustee of the IRA for proper accounting, reporting and custody of the assets.

Assume the IRA owner did not guarantee the debt, and the IRA still does not have enough cash to make the next loan payment. If the owner has not already made the maximum allowable IRA contribution for that year, she may make a contribution to the account in cash which can be used by the IRA to make the loan payment.[6] This option is limited to the annual contribution limits imposed on IRAs. The current contribution limits are $5,000 for an IRA owner under age 50, and $6,000 for owners age 50 and up.

---

[4] IRC 408(a)(2) & 408(h)

[5] IRC 408(a)(1)

[6] Another possible solution may be for the account owner to loan funds to the IRA under the guidance of Department of Labor Prohibited Transaction Exemption 80-26. A full discussion of this exemption is beyond the scope of this book and professional advice should be sought before relying on this exemption.

Unrelated Business Income Tax (UBIT)

Advisors and IRA owners are hard wired to automatically believe all investment activity within an IRA is tax protected. And most of the time it is. However, certain investments and actions by an IRA trigger the UBIT rules and subject a portion of IRA earnings to tax.[7]

The term unrelated business taxable income (UBTI) refers to earnings received by an IRA that are subject to tax. The tax is generally referred to as the unrelated business income tax (UBIT). So, UBTI is the income that triggers the tax, which is UBIT. One of the most common forms of UBTI is known as Unrelated Debt Financed Income (UDFI).[8] That's a lot of acronyms! UDFI is income derived as a result of using debt within the IRA to increase the funds available for investment. The amount of income subject to tax is roughly the same proportion as the amount of debt to equity in the investment.[9]

For example, Tom's IRA buys a rental house with sixty percent down and forty percent financing. Forty percent of the net rental income is considered related to the debt financed portion of the property and thus subject to tax. In this case, Tom's IRA custodian must file a special tax return (Form 990-T) for his IRA to report the UBTI and have the IRA pay the proper amount of tax.

It is important to note that IRAs are treated the same as other taxpayers in these situations. As such, the IRA can deduct the same types of normal business expenses that an individual

---

[7] IRC 408(e)(1)

[8] Please note there are many scenarios which can create other types of UBTI within an IRA. However, this text only deals with the type known as UDFI.

[9] IRC 514(a)(1)

or corporation may deduct.[10] These include things such as investment interest, depreciation, repairs and maintenance, advertising, property management, utilities, insurance, property taxes and so on. The amount deducted is proportionate to the amount of debt involved.[11] There is also a statutory exemption for the first $1,000 of UBTI.[12] For example, an IRA with UBTI of $10,000 after deducting all expenses will only be subject to tax on $9,000 due to this exemption.

At first glance, it may seem counterproductive to create a scenario where an IRA would owe tax on its earnings. However, the advantages of using debt to increase investment opportunity are similar to a non-IRA investor. If the IRA can use leverage to gain access to better and bigger investment opportunities and earn excess return over the cost of the loan (interest, UBIT, etc.), it wins. Disregarding the potential use of debt to help build IRA profits is akin to saying no one should buy rental property unless they can pay all cash for the deal.

Prohibited Transactions

The two most common forms of PTs found in IRAs using debt are when the IRA borrows funds from a disqualified person and when the IRA owner guarantees the debt personally. For example, Daughter's IRA has $50,000. Mother lends $25,000 to the IRA to purchase a rental property and charges a fair market interest rate as evidenced by a formal promissory note. The formalities of the transaction such as a promissory note, adequate interest rate and legitimate investment purpose are irrelevant. The transaction is a PT and triggers the consequences of such solely because Mother is a disqualified person with respect to Daughter's IRA.

---

[10] IRC 514(a)(3)

[11] IRC 514(a)(2)

[12] IRC 512(b)(12)

The other common PT where the IRA owner guarantees the debt is sometimes harder to spot. Often the IRA owner applies for a loan through a lender intending to own the property in their IRA. The IRA supplies the down payment. In the natural course of making the loan, the lender uses their typical paperwork that includes a personal guarantee by the IRA owner. The IRA owner signs all the documents unwittingly having made a PT by signing the guarantee form.

Another common mistake is when the loan is made to the IRA owner as the borrower and guarantor directly. In other words, the IRA never appears on any of the loan documents. For example, Jacob applies for a loan from his local bank to buy a rental property. The bank uses his credit and financial information to approve the loan and issues the loan to Jacob in his name. Jacob takes funds from his IRA to cover the down payment. However, the deed is recorded with Jacob as the legal owner of the property, not his IRA. Jacob falsely believes the property is owned by his IRA because that was his intent. He later forwards all rental income to the IRA custodian for deposit. In reality, the down payment money withdrawn from the IRA was a taxable distribution and should have been reported in the year withdrawn.

It is imperative that an IRA owner ensure:

- The IRA does not borrow funds from a disqualified person.
- The IRA owner does not personally guarantee the debt of the IRA.
- The transaction is a true arms-length deal between authorized third parties.
- The documents including the recorded deed are properly vested in the legal name of the IRA.

- That the IRA will have sufficient cash on hand to cover debt service at times when there is little or no rental income.

For more information on Prohibited Transactions, see Chapter Two.

Chapter Eighteen

Leveraged IRA Roth Conversions

We've already reviewed the incredible tax saving power available when an IRA holds assets subject to discount valuation adjustments. It is hard to believe those results could actually be improved upon *let alone doubled*. Such is the added power when using leverage within an IRA.

Case Study – Sharon Uses Leverage to Do a Larger Real Estate Transaction

Sharon's traditional IRA has $1,000,000. She found a very attractive real estate opportunity requiring $2,000,000. If she can get the funds, her IRA will purchase a minority interest in a real estate limited partnership (LP) that has acquired the rights to a large tract of land ideal for development. The time frame to complete development is estimated at five years. Based on the general partner's track record on these types of deals, and Sharon and her advisors' detailed analysis of the opportunity, it looks like her IRA could reap substantial profit over the life of the deal.

Sharon's IRA obtains a nonrecourse loan for $1,000,000 in order to meet the $2,000,000 investment amount. The loan is interest only with a balloon payment due in five years. So the IRA only has to pay the annual interest on the note during the five year property development period when there is no income being produced by the investment. The IRA has sufficient extra cash available to meet the interest payments when due.

However, for simplicity in numbers, we will review the IRA as though the LP interest and nonrecourse debt are the only assets and liabilities of the account.

Here is the net value of Sharon's IRA after obtaining the loan but just prior to purchasing the LP interest:

IRA Cash on Hand	$ 2,000,000
Minus liabilities	- (1,000,000)
IRA FMV	**$ 1,000,000**

After the LP interest is owned by the IRA, the value equation changes considerably. The typical discounting factors reviewed previously must be considered when determining the FMV of the IRA's minority interest in the LP.

Six months after the investment is made, Sharon's advisors recommend she consider a Roth conversion of her traditional IRA. A qualified appraiser is retained to provide a FMV of the IRA's LP interest. The valuation report shows a thirty percent discount from the $2,000,000 NAV. Here is the tax result of doing the Roth conversion:

Table 14

LP Interest NAV	$2,000,000
Valuation Adjustment	30%
LP Interest FMV	$1,400,000
Liabilities	($1,000,000)
IRA FMV	$400,000
Income Tax on Conversion[1]	($160,000)

---

[1] Assumes combined state and federal income tax bracket of 40%.

The tax owed is only $160,000! If Sharon had done the Roth conversion while holding the original $1,000,000 cash, the cost would have been $400,000 using the same tax rate.

One of the most amazing facts in this scenario is the effective tax rate. Based on her original IRA NAV of $1,000,000, the effective tax rate is only sixteen percent![2] Sharon paid tax at the full forty percent rate required, but she only had to pay on $400,000 of taxable income rather than $1,000,000. When looking back to her original IRA NAV, we see she only paid sixteen percent of that amount in tax. The tax would have been $240,000 higher if Sharon had done her Roth conversion with $1,000,000 cash in the IRA.

Table Fifteen shows the side-by-side comparison between keeping the traditional IRA versus converting to Roth. This analysis assumes the following:

- The real estate project in Sharon's IRA doubles in value over five years.[3]
- The LP investors are cashed out after five years as planned.
- Sharon's IRA repays the principal outstanding on the loan.
- Sharon qualifies for tax-free treatment of Roth IRA withdrawals.
- Non-IRA assets available to pay tax on conversion - $160,000
- Annual growth rate on non-IRA assets – 6%

---

[2] $160,000 tax / $1,000,000 IRA NAV = 16% effective tax rate.

[3] Annualized rate of gain equal to 14.87% compounded.

Table 15

	Traditional IRA w/ Leverage	Roth Conversion w/ Leverage
Future IRA NAV	$4,000,000	$4,000,000
IRA Liabilities	($1,000,000)	($1,000,000)
Future IRA FMV	$3,000,000	$3,000,000
Non-IRA assets	$160,000	$160,000
Tax on Roth conversion[4]	N/A	($160,000)
Future value of non-IRA assets[5]	$214,000	$0
Tax on IRA withdrawal[6]	($1,200,000)	N/A
Net remaining after tax	$2,014,000	$3,000,000
Net tax advantage of Roth conversion	--	**+$986,000**

This begs the question outlined in Chapter Seven earlier: how likely is it that Sharon will ever be in a tax bracket lower than sixteen percent later in life when she begins taking withdrawals from her traditional IRA? Not likely at all. In order to pay just $160,000 in tax on the $3,000,000 traditional IRA shown in

---

[4] Assumes Roth conversion occurs before growth with tax owed on $400,000 of FMV ($2 million NAV- 30% discount - $1 million liability = $400k FMV) for the w/ leverage scenario as shown in Table 14.

[5] Future value of non-IRA assets is $0 in the Roth column because these funds were used to pay tax on the conversion.

[6] Assumes combined state and federal income tax bracket of 40% for traditional IRA. No tax is due on the Roth IRA withdrawals.

Table Fifteen, the effective tax rate would need to be just five and one third percent (5.33%)! And remember, that's a combined state and federal tax rate. I'm willing to go on record right now predicting there will never be a time when U.S. income tax rates on $3,000,000 of taxable income will be less than six percent.

Let's be even more optimistic and use the same growth rate on the non-IRA assets as we did on the IRA assets. In that case, the $160,000 would double to $320,000. This would improve the traditional IRA side of the table quite a bit. However, the Roth conversion side would still be ahead by $880,000!

In the example from Table Fifteen, loan interest and UBIT on the capital gain, if applicable, are equal in both cases and thus not relevant factors. However, we must consider their effects when comparing a leveraged Roth conversion to a non-leveraged conversion or simply keeping a non-leveraged traditional IRA. UBIT applies to capital gains in cases where the debt was in place up to twelve months prior to the sale or other capital gain recognition event.

Assume Sharon's IRA loan is at five percent. The current prime rate in the U.S. as of this writing is three and one quarter percent (3.25%). The IRA will make total interest payments of $250,000.[7] One half of the capital gain would be considered UDFI/UBTI since that is the ratio of debt to equity. The IRA

---

[7] 5yr loan term x $50,000 annual interest payments = $250,000.

will owe $150,000 of tax.[8] The total combined cost of UBIT and loan interest is $400,000. Adding in the tax on the Roth conversion brings the total expense to $560,000. That sounds worse than just doing the conversion on the original $1,000,000 IRA and paying $400,000 of tax in the first place. Table Sixteen compares the two Roth conversion scenarios using the same growth rate for both:

---

[8] $1,000,000 capital gain x 15% current federal long term capital gain tax rate. Note the calculation of UBIT in this scenario has been simplified. Several other factors may apply to reduce this tax including the possible deduction of loan interest, the statutory exemption amount, etc.

Table 16

	Roth Conversion w/o Leverage	Roth Conversion w/ Leverage
Future IRA NAV	$2,000,000	$4,000,000
IRA liabilities	N/A	($1,000,000)
Future IRA FMV	$2,000,000	$3,000,000
Non-IRA assets	$400,000	$400,000
Tax on Roth conversion[9]	($400,000)	($160,000)
Future value of non-IRA assets[10]	$0	$321,000
Loan interest	N/A	($250,000)
UBIT	N/A	($150,000)
Net total value	$2,000,000	$2,921,000
Net advantage of IRA w/ leverage	--	**+$921,000**

[9] Assumes Roth conversion occurs before growth with tax owed on $1 million of FMV for the w/o leverage scenario and on $400,000 of FMV ($2 million NAV – 30% discount - $1 million liability = $400k FMV) for the w/ leverage scenario as shown in Table 14.

[10] Future value of non-IRA assets is $0 in the left column because these funds were used to pay tax on the conversion. The right column reflects funds remaining after paying the Roth conversion tax grown at six percent per year ($400k-$160k=$240k; $240k @ 6% for 5yrs=$321k).

Sharon's net advantage of doing the Roth conversion combined with the leveraged real estate transaction is almost $1,000,000 when compared to just converting her existing IRA portfolio to a Roth IRA. This advantage exists even after deducting for loan interest and UBIT.

What if the real estate project in Sharon's IRA does not double in value and only returns one percent over the entire five year time horizon? That's only zero point two percent (0.2%) annually over five years and would be considered a horrible investment. Instinctively, we might assume such a scenario would cause the traditional IRA without leverage to come out ahead of the leveraged Roth conversion. Table Seventeen shows the results of each side-by-side:

Table 17

	Traditional IRA w/o Leverage	Roth Conversion w/ Leverage
Future IRA NAV	$1,010,000	$2,020,000
IRA Liabilities	N/A	($1,000,000)
Future IRA FMV	$1,010,000	$1,020,000
Non-IRA assets	$160,000	$160,000
Tax on Roth conversion[11]	N/A	($160,000)
Future value of non-IRA assets[12]	$161,600	$0
Tax on IRA withdrawal[13]	($404,000)	N/A
Loan interest	N/A	($250,000)
UBIT	N/A	($1,500)
Net remaining after expenses	$767,600	$768,500
Net advantage	--	**+$900**

[11] Assumes Roth conversion occurs before growth with tax owed on $400,000 of FMV ($2 million NAV – 30% discount - $1 million liability = $400k FMV) for the w/ leverage scenario as shown in Table 14.

[12] Future value of non-IRA assets is $0 in the Roth column because these funds were used to pay tax on the conversion. Value in traditional IRA column reflects total growth of 1% as used for the IRA assets.

[13] Assumes combined state and federal income tax bracket of 40% for traditional IRA. No tax is due on the Roth IRA withdrawals.

Wow! The leveraged Roth conversion beats holding the traditional IRA even at less than one quarter of one percent annual growth and five percent loan interest over five years. The advantage becomes more significant as the growth rate on the IRA assets increases.

Chapter Nineteen

Private Investment Funds: Attractive Assets for Leveraged IRAs

The case study in Chapter Eighteen shows the possibilities of using leverage in a real estate transaction which is often the most common application. However, the same principles and results apply to other assets subject to discount valuation. IRAs can borrow funds for any legitimate investment purpose including hedge funds, private investment funds (PIFs), private REITS, private equity transactions or funds, etc.

In fact, properly structured PIFs may provide the most flexibility and predictability of all the options. A PIF is generally structured as a LP or LLC. Multiple investors own units or interests in the company which manages the collective capital for mutual gain and profit. Each PIF typically has a specified investment objective similar to those found in traditional mutual funds such as large-cap growth, growth with income, international, emerging markets, international fixed income, etc. PIFs often have a predetermined time horizon or lifespan of a period of years. For example, a PIF may have a designated liquidation date after three years when the units become fully liquid to the investors. Investors must hold their interest until such a date with limited or no opportunity to convert their interest to cash. This maintains portfolio integrity allowing the manager(s) to use their best ideas over a specified time horizon without concern over liquidity constraints.

The specified liquidity date can make a PIF more attractive than a real estate transaction, hedge fund or other illiquid asset with an unknown time horizon. This is especially true when an IRA uses debt to fund part of its investment. It is important for the IRA owner and the lender to know how long the funds must be tied up before they can be converted back into cash to repay the loan. PIFs with specified time horizons may be more attractive to both the lender and IRA owner.

PIFs also commonly invest in marketable securities which are generally easy to liquidate upon PIF termination. This may provide additional comfort to lenders and IRA owners by removing three additional risks:

1. Cash to repay the loan: A loan secured by real estate that comes due in three years may be in jeopardy if the underlying real estate cannot be sold at the appropriate time. A PIF with a three year time horizon holding marketable securities generally will not incur a liquidity problem upon termination. The lender is assured that cash will be available from the PIF liquidation leaving only the risk of whether the NAV has increased, decreased or remained constant over the life of the loan and investment.

2. "Predictable" returns: Technically, there is no such thing as a predictable return and lenders must consider the risk of the collateral. For example, an IRA borrowing money to invest in a startup hair salon is arguably riskier than borrowing to invest in a PIF holding a diversified portfolio of large-cap international stocks and bonds. A lender can review past performance, manager tenure, portfolio construction, philosophy, expenses and any number of other data points to become more comfortable with a proposed PIF investment.

3. Simple to "foreclose": It is much easier to retitle investment funds held in an account as security for a loan than it is to foreclose on real estate or hard assets. This provides protection to the lender in the event the IRA defaults on its loan obligation. The lender simply has the PIF units retitled per the collateral agreement. One banker suggested to me that these types of loans might be considered "cash secured" which carry less risk to a bank.

Therefore, a PIF with a known time horizon, liquidation date and transparent investment approach can often be very attractive in these scenarios. In the Chapter Eighteen case study, the real estate partnership was expected to liquidate in five years and the balloon payment on the note was also due in five years. However, there was real risk to the IRA and the lender if the real estate deal took longer than expected or could not be sold for sufficient value at that time. This exact scenario was common for real estate developers, investors and lenders during the real estate crisis of the last few years. PIFs eliminate this risk and thus allow the IRA loan to be tailored with a balloon payment at just the right time when the PIF converts to cash.

Chapter Twenty

Tax Savings on Other Leveraged IRA Transactions

The IRA case study reviewed in Chapter Eighteen highlighted the tax savings potential of a Roth conversion while holding leveraged and discounted assets. Similar results from combining leverage with discounted assets are also possible in all the other IRA scenarios shown in Part Two.

To make the math easy and enhance understanding, all examples in Chapters Twenty-one through Twenty-four reflect IRAs borrowing fifty percent of the total investment amount and contributing the other fifty percent as equity. It is important to note similar positive tax savings can be obtained using leverage of different amounts. For example, in some cases an IRA may put up seventy percent and borrow thirty percent or vice versa.

The following chapters outline brief examples and summaries of various scenarios where discounted assets combined with leverage in the IRA can significantly boost tax savings. Each of these cases assumes the same set of facts as the case study from Chapter Eighteen previously:

- Traditional IRA with $2,000,000 NAV made up of $1,000,000 principal and $1,000,000 borrowed funds (fifty percent debt to equity ratio).
- Assets discounted by thirty percent making the adjusted NAV $1,400,000.
- FMV of $400,000 after deducting the $1,000,000 liability of the IRA.

Chapter Twenty-One

Leveraged IRA Distributions

The tax result from converting ordinary income to capital gains is significant as shown in Chapter Eleven. It is even better when leverage is applied inside the IRA. A full distribution of the IRA described in Chapter Twenty results in $400,000 of ordinary income at the time of distribution which becomes the tax basis for the asset(s) going forward. Assuming no change in value, upon liquidation and loan repayment the asset would be worth $1,000,000 made up of $400,000 of basis and $600,000 of capital gain. Table Eighteen shows the net tax benefit of this transaction compared to distributing the original $1,000,000 of IRA assets:

Table 18

	Distribution at Full NAV	Distribution w/ Reduced FMV
IRA NAV	$1,000,000	$2,000,000
Valuation Adjustment	N/A	30%
Minus liabilities	N/A	($1,000,000)
IRA FMV	$1,000,000	$400,000
OI Tax[1] on Distribution	($400,000)	($160,000)
LTCG Tax[2] on $600k discount	N/A	($90,000)
Total Tax	($400,000)	($250,000)
Net Tax Advantage	--	**+$150,000**

---

[1] Ordinary income tax using assumed combined state and federal tax bracket of 40%.

[2] Long term capital gains tax at 15%.

The transaction described significantly reduces the total tax owed on the IRA. It also allows the IRA owner to potentially decide the timing of the capital gain recognition assuming the asset does not have a particular liquidation date. Capital gains are not recognized for tax purposes until the asset is sold. This adds flexibility for future tax planning. The IRA owner may want to sell the asset and incur the taxable gain in a year when she has other capital losses. Or perhaps she waits until she has a low income year, tax rates are more favorable or in combination with a large charitable gift deduction. Depending on estate tax laws in effect at the time of her death, and assuming she still holds the distributed asset, her heirs may even receive a step up in basis. In that event, the new basis would be $1,000,000 (assuming no change in value between the date of distribution and date of death). The heirs could theoretically liquidate the asset for $1,000,000 and incur zero capital gains tax. Some investments have provisions allowing for full liquidation of shares in the event of the original owner's death as mentioned in Chapter Fourteen.

Chapter Twenty-Two

Reducing RMDs with Leveraged IRA Assets

As outlined earlier, RMDs, when required, are calculated based on the total value of the IRA as of December 31st each year. The total FMV is divided by the applicable factor from either Table I (Single Life Expectancy), Table II (Joint Life and Last Survivor Expectancy) or Table III (Uniform Lifetime).[1] A lower IRA value results in a lower required distribution and thus less taxable income to report.

Table Nineteen shows the different RMDs for a 75 year old IRA owner using the Table III life expectancy factor applied to each of these three scenarios:

- NAV = FMV = $1,000,000
- 30% discount to NAV = $700,000 FMV
- Leverage + 30% discount to NAV = $400,000 FMV

Table 19

	FMV	LE Factor[2]	RMD[3]
IRA 1	$1,000,000	22.9	$43,700
IRA 2	$700,000	22.9	$30,600
IRA 3	$400,000	22.9	$17,500

---

[1] All three tables are found in Appendices A, B and C, respectively.

[2] Life expectancy factor.

[3] Amounts rounded to nearest $100.

The leveraged IRA scenario allows for a sixty percent reduction in the required distribution *which means sixty percent less taxable income to report.* This technique can be very useful in cases where the desire is to maximize and maintain IRA assets as long as possible and minimize current taxable income.

Chapter Twenty-Three

The Super – Super Stretch IRA

Chapter Thirteen reviewed the concept of a stretch IRA allowing a beneficiary to prolong the life of the tax protected funds over their life expectancy. This opportunity becomes even more powerful when combined with leverage inside the IRA.

Case Study – Son Inherits VERY Large Roth IRA

Daniel was a successful businessman. At the time of his death, he had a Roth IRA valued at $20,000,000. That sounds like a lot for a Roth IRA considering they've only been around since 1998. In this case, Daniel had built the account through a combination of contributions and rollovers from other plans. But the real value came from a few very significant investment picks that ended up shooting the lights out. A $20,000,000 IRA is a big deal by itself. A $20,000,000 Roth IRA is an amazing deal! That's a whole lot of tax-free money and the potential for huge gains over time – all tax-free.

Dan Jr. inherited the Roth IRA and was required to start taking RMDs when he was twenty-five years old. Luckily, Dan Jr. had very good professional advisors helping him sort through the investment and tax issues associated with this account. They advised him to stretch the IRA over his lifetime by taking only the minimum required distribution each year. This would allow the account to continue to grow tax-free over his lifetime. However, even the minimum distributions on an account that size are several hundred thousand dollars. They began to look for solutions to reduce the amount of annual required distributions since Dan Jr. did not need the full amount, and each dollar kept in the account could continue to compound tax-free.

Table Twenty shows the difference in RMDs between these three scenarios:

1. NAV = FMV = $20,000,000
2. 30% discount to NAV = $14,000,000 FMV
3. Leverage + 30% discount to NAV = $8,000,000 FMV

Table 20

	FMV	LE Factor[1]	RMD[2]
IRA 1	$20,000,000	58.2	$343,600
IRA 2	$14,000,000	58.2	$240,500
IRA 3	$8,000,000	58.2	$137,500

Whether you have a multi-million dollar IRA or a one hundred thousand dollar IRA, the net effect is the same. Using leverage combined with discounted assets significantly reduces the RMD and allows the bulk of the assets to grow tax protected in the IRA for many years.

---

[1] Table I Life Expectancy factor for 25 year old beneficiary. See Appendix A.

[2] Amounts rounded to nearest $100.

Chapter Twenty-Four

Leveraged IRAs
Minimize Estate Tax

E state tax is based on the FMV of the decedent's assets, including IRAs, at the time of death or six months later on what is called the alternate valuation date.[1] Thus a lower value equates to less tax owed.

As we've already seen, leveraged IRAs holding assets subject to valuation discounts can achieve very large reductions in FMV. These reductions can translate into very large estate tax savings keeping more money in the tax protected account and leaving a larger legacy for the family or charity. Table Twenty-one shows a side-by-side comparison of an IRA with and without leverage being subject to estate tax:

Table 21

	IRA at Full NAV	Leveraged IRA w/ Discounted FMV
IRA NAV	$1,000,000	$2,000,000
Valuation adjustment	N/A	30%
Minus liabilities	N/A	($1,000,000)
IRA FMV	$1,000,000	$400,000
Estate tax (35%)	($350,000)	($140,000)
Net Tax Advantage		**+$210,000**

---

[1] IRC 2032

That's a huge estate tax savings at the thirty-five percent rate. At the 2013 estate tax rate of fifty-five percent, the amount saved jumps to $330,000!

Recall from the previous estate tax discussion that the combination of estate tax plus income tax to the beneficiary can cause substantial IRA value erosion. In fact, the net value to the beneficiary was roughly a third of the original IRA value after applying the thirty-five percent estate tax and forty percent estimated income tax. Compare that with the example below showing the effect of estate and income tax on a leveraged inherited IRA holding discounted assets:

Traditional IRA NAV	$ 2,000,000
Traditional IRA FMV	$ 400,000
Estate tax	$ (140,000)
Income tax[2]	$ (104,000)
Net to beneficiary[3]	**$ 756,000**

The net amount to the beneficiary is almost double that of the non-leveraged and non-discounted IRA ($390,000 vs. $756,000).

---

[2] Assumes assets distributed in kind with $400,000 FMV as taxable income and applies the Section 691(c) deduction allowed for the estate tax paid above.

[3] Reflects full NAV minus liabilities and estate and income tax paid.

Chapter Twenty-Five

TAX-FREE Distributions & Roth Conversions (Really!)

If you've made it this far, your head is probably reeling with information and ideas or... you saw the title of this chapter and jumped ahead!

First, we looked at tax savings opportunities for IRA transactions simply by properly valuing the assets held in the IRA. Next, we looked at how leverage within the IRA can enhance those tax reductions. This chapter shows how putting it all together just right can eliminate the tax bite altogether.

We know from prior chapters that traditional IRA distributions and Roth conversions are taxable events and subject to ordinary income tax rates. The amount subject to tax is equal to the FMV of the assets being distributed or converted. The question is: at what FMV does the distribution or conversion result in zero tax liability? The answer is in the question: zero. If a traditional IRA with a FMV of $0 is converted to a Roth IRA, no tax is owed. Zero taxable income results in zero tax. The same is true of a distribution from a traditional IRA. If the FMV is $0, the tax owed is $0.

How can an IRA asset ever be worth nothing without actually being worthless? The answer is in the mathematics behind discounting combined with leverage. I know, you thought we already covered that. We did, but I saved the really good stuff for this chapter with the catchier title.

Here's the secret: if the amount of discount on an asset is equal to or greater than the IRA's equity in the asset, the FMV is zero.

Table Twenty-two shows the FMV as a percentage of gross NAV for various combinations of discount and IRA equity percentages:

Table 22

		% Valuation Adjustment (Discount)				
		10	20	30	40	50
% IRA Equity	10	0	0	0	0	0
	20	10%	0	0	0	0
	30	20%	10%	0	0	0
	40	30%	20%	10%	0	0
	50	40%	30%	20%	10%	0

FMV as a % of NAV

Case Study – Amy's IRA Buys
Private Biotech Shares

Amy has an IRA worth $300,000. Her IRA borrows $700,000 in order to make a combined total investment of $1,000,000 into a promising biotechnology company. The company is privately held, and Amy's IRA buys the shares as part of a private placement transaction. Several months after the investment, Amy's tax advisors recommend she consider a Roth conversion. A qualified appraiser is retained to determine the appropriate FMV since the biotech company shares are not liquid and do not trade on an established exchange. The valuation report shows a thirty percent valuation adjustment (discount) from her original purchase price. Table Twenty-three shows the new FMV calculation for Amy's IRA:

Table 23

Biotech shares NAV	$1,000,000
Valuation adjustment	30%
Biotech shares FMV	$700,000
Minus IRA liabilities	($700,000)
IRA FMV	$0

Can the value of the IRA really be nothing? Absolutely! Look at the scenario from another angle. Assume Amy's IRA decides to sell its biotech company shares. What would an outside investor pay for those shares? We already know from the appraisal report that the IRA will need to drop the price from $1,000,000 down to $700,000 in order to realistically entice a buyer. This is similar to the example shown in Chapter Four where Kevin must drop the price of his interest in the dry cleaning business to attract buyers. If the IRA sells its shares for $700,000 cash, it has just enough money to repay the debt leaving nothing leftover in the IRA. So the net FMV of the IRA is truly $0 in this example.

At this point Amy can do her Roth conversion tax-free. She could also take a full tax-free distribution of her IRA. Interestingly, if Amy took a full IRA distribution at this point she would also avoid the ten percent penalty tax if she is under age 59 ½. The ten percent penalty tax applied to zero taxable income results in no tax owed.

In reality, the exact amounts of IRA equity and valuation adjustment will vary and may never be equal. However, if the discount percentage is greater than the IRA equity percentage, the net result is still a FMV of $0. If the discount percentage is less than the IRA equity percentage, the results are still significant. For comparison purposes, Table Twenty-four shows Amy's IRA where the valuation adjustment is slightly less than her IRA equity percentage (25% discount vs. 30% IRA equity):

Table 24

Biotech shares NAV	$1,000,000
Valuation adjustment	25%
Biotech shares FMV	$750,000
Minus IRA liabilities	($700,000)
IRA FMV	$50,000

Obviously, a Roth conversion or IRA distribution at $50,000 of taxable value is much better than one at her original value of $300,000. The tax savings assuming a forty percent combined state and federal tax rate is $100,000.[1]

---

[1] Tax on $50,000 at 40% = $20,000; tax on $300,000 at 40% = $120,000.

In practical application, if the IRA FMV was $0 as in Table Twenty-three, Amy would probably contribute at least a minimal amount of cash to the account. This serves two purposes. First, it ensures the custodian will keep the account open. If the custodian determines the IRA to have a FMV of $0, it may attempt to close the account. Second, it ensures the custodian will report at least some amount of taxable conversion or distribution value. They are not required to issue Form 1099-R if the asset/account is worthless at the time of distribution.[2] However, showing some value on the Form 1099-R and reporting it as taxable income starts the statute of limitations running which limits the amount of time the IRS has to argue over the valuation report from Amy's appraiser.[3]

Why would Amy continue to keep the IRA if its FMV was $0? Naturally, Amy is hoping the biotech company investment will generate significant returns over time. The IRA still owns the shares even though its FMV reflects no value when the discounts and liabilities are taken into account.

Assume Amy went through with the Roth conversion at the recommendation of her advisors. She paid effectively zero tax other than perhaps some nominal amount based on a small cash position contributed to the account as described above. She now has a Roth IRA with the same FMV ($0) as the traditional IRA had prior to the conversion. Five years later, the biotech company develops some very promising new medical devices and is bought buy a large multinational pharmaceutical company at a large premium. Amy's Roth IRA receives $2,000,000 for its shares. After repaying the debt, Amy's IRA has $1,300,000

[2] IRS *2011 Instructions for Forms 1099-R and 5498*, pgs. 1 & 8

[3] See Chapter Sixteen – Risks.

in cash (remember she started with $300,000). The account is a Roth IRA, so the entire $1,300,000 is tax-free.[4] Amy has effectively created $1,300,000 of completely tax-free money since she didn't even have to pay tax on the Roth conversion.

Some of you reading this are shaking the book right about now and shouting: "what about the loan interest and possible UBIT?!" In the case study shown, it is very likely that cumulative loan interest and UBIT on the sale of the biotech company shares will be higher than the tax saved on the Roth conversion. If loan interest was five percent as in a previous example, Amy's IRA would pay $175,000 over the life of the loan.[5] If UBIT applied to the capital gain as in our previous example, Amy's IRA would owe $105,000 in tax.[6] The total outlay comes to $280,000. At first glance, this seems like a bad deal compared to only saving $120,000 in tax on the Roth conversion.[7]

However, that isn't the right question to ask and is actually irrelevant. Amy and her advisors identified an attractive investment opportunity in the biotech company and arranged to make a $1,000,000 investment using her traditional IRA. This required her IRA to borrow additional funds since it only had $300,000 to start. *So Amy's IRA was ALWAYS going to incur loan interest and UBIT whether she converted to a Roth IRA or not!* Since the loan interest and UBIT costs are identical in both

---

[4] Provided distributions meet the criteria for tax-free treatment found in IRC 408A(d).

[5] 5yr loan term x $35,000 annual interest payments = $175,000.

[6] $700,000 UDFI portion of capital gain x 15% current federal long-term capital gains tax rate.

[7] Assumes combined state and federal income tax bracket of 40% applied to the original IRA value of $300,000.

scenarios (traditional IRA and Roth conversion) we can ignore these expenses. They have the same effect in either case.

The true comparison is whether the Roth conversion saved her taxes over the long haul. It very clearly did. If she held the traditional IRA and ended up with $1.02 million after deducting $280,000 for UBIT and loan interest, the income tax would have been $408,000 assuming a forty percent combined state and federal rate. Instead, she ended up with $1.02 million in a Roth IRA tax-free, effectively saving over four hundred thousand dollars of tax.

Case Study – Jim's IRA is Drowning

The huge drop in real estate values nationwide has caused many properties to be "underwater." Underwater refers to the situation when a property's value is less than the current mortgage debt on the property.

Jim purchased a single family rental home with his traditional IRA for $150,000 during the real estate boom. His IRA made a down payment of $60,000 (forty percent) and financed the remaining $90,000 (sixty percent) using an appropriately structured nonrecourse loan. The mortgage was for thirty years at eight percent interest with monthly payments of $660. The property rents for $1300 per month. After all expenses, Jim's IRA nets $3600 per year in free cash flow. This equals a six percent annualized cash flow or cash-on-cash return based on his original $60,000 down payment. Six percent is a very attractive yield currently and has the potential to increase over time as rental rates increase and the mortgage debt is paid down.

Luckily for Jim, rental rates are not tied to property values in his area because the value of the property has decreased significantly. The property decreased in value by fifty percent in the two years following his IRA purchase. Similar homes are now selling for only $75,000.

Here is Jim's current IRA value:

Current property value	$ 75,000
Liabilities[8]	-$(88,400)
IRA FMV	**$ 0**

This is a classic example of a property underwater. The principal on the loan is more than $13,000 higher than the property is worth. However, the property still produces positive cash flow at a very attractive rate based on the original principal put into the deal by the IRA (six percent). There is little risk of the IRA defaulting on the loan with such strong rental income, and Jim expects to hold the property in his IRA for many years. This will help correct the underwater mortgage situation as the loan is paid down and property values begin to recover over time.

In the meantime, however, Jim's IRA has an effective FMV of zero. This provides an excellent opportunity to convert the account to a Roth IRA with no tax liability. Then all future income and capital appreciation within the account are completely tax-free under the Roth IRA rules. Anyone that made a similar investment with their IRA in the last several years would be wise to review the current property and mortgage values and consider a Roth conversion if circumstances are favorable.

---

[8] Principal balance remaining on mortgage after two years rounded to nearest $100.

Also note that if Jim's IRA sold the property for the current value of $75,000, the amount of recognized loss is the difference between the cost basis (generally the purchase price with applicable adjustments) and the amount of nonrecourse debt outstanding (mortgage balance).[9] The tax code states that for purposes of determining gain or loss, FMV of an *asset* subject to nonrecourse indebtedness cannot be less than the outstanding debt remaining. To avoid confusion, please note the rule is that FMV of the asset cannot be less than the outstanding nonrecourse debt *when determining gain or loss* on a transaction. To properly determine the FMV of the overall *account*, custodians must still deduct the liabilities of the IRA. Thus, even in the absence of a gain/loss event, assuming one uses an asset FMV equal to the outstanding nonrecourse debt, the FMV of Jim's IRA is still zero. In this example, it would mean using an asset FMV of $88,400 instead of the appraised value of $75,000. The result is still an IRA FMV of zero ($88,400 deemed FMV - $88,400 liability = $0).

As noted earlier, some practitioners downplay the opportunity to convert traditional IRAs to Roth IRAs due to the effects of paying large tax bills upfront. *But there is no advantage to holding a traditional IRA if it can be converted to a Roth IRA tax-free.* Even practitioners who are not enamored with Roth conversions will admit there is some level of tax where a conversion is the best choice. Imagine an IRA owner in the thirty-five percent federal tax bracket who declines a Roth conversion because thirty-five percent of the account value is too high a price to pay. Would he convert if the tax was only twenty-five percent? How about fifteen percent? Five percent? And of course, there is no rational argument against converting if the

---

[9] IRC 7701(g)

transaction is free (zero tax). Even the most ardent supporters of maintaining traditional IRAs to the bitter end become Roth conversion cheerleaders when the tax bill is reduced low enough.

PART FOUR

Creditor Protection & Bankruptcy

Chapter Twenty-Six

Protecting IRAs from Creditors

(WARNING: This is an extremely complicated area of law subject to many changes including past cases and court opinions that often alter the rules. You must seek professional advice if you are in a situation where creditor issues or bankruptcy are involved.)

Creditor protection for IRAs is generally a function of state law and differs substantially from state to state. There is also an entirely different set of laws related to IRA protection in cases of bankruptcy by the IRA owner.

It is beyond the scope of this book to delve into the different laws of all 50 states and the corresponding case law history of each. Instead, we will review the federal bankruptcy rules pertaining to IRAs and use Nevada as a case study state for non-bankruptcy situations.

Federal Bankruptcy Rules Pertaining to IRAs

Certain property is considered exempt from the property of the estate during bankruptcy proceedings.[1] Property that falls under an exemption is not considered an asset of the debtor when determining how to reimburse creditors and settle the bankruptcy case. There are exemptions for things ranging from household furnishings to tools of the trade of the debtor to retirement accounts.

---

[1] 11 U.S.C. 522

IRAs are covered in three sections of the Bankruptcy Code.[2] The rules are different depending on where the assets in the IRA originated. Assets rolled over to an IRA from true ERISA plans such as group 401(k) plans, pension plans, etc. are one category. Assets and earnings accumulated in IRAs and Roth IRAs from direct contributions by the IRA owner are another category. Rollover assets are exempt with no limits on how much value is protected. Contributed assets and their earnings are subject to a cap of $1,000,000. However, this amount is indexed for inflation and adjusts every three years on April 1st.[3] The most recent adjustment was in 2010, when the exempt amount was raised to $1,171,650.[4]

FMV is the required value when calculating the total IRA balance to determine if the value is more or less than the exemption amount.[5] Thus, proper valuation of IRA assets can be very important to debtors in bankruptcy proceedings. Consider an IRA with a NAV of $1,500,000. If the NAV and FMV are equal (i.e. IRA holds all cash), then the IRA owner could lose up to $328,350 from the IRA in a bankruptcy proceeding. This excess amount above the exemption threshold of $1,171,650 is subject to attachment/seizure/forfeiture to satisfy outstanding debts. Consider the same IRA holding assets subject to a twenty five percent discount valuation adjustment from NAV. The FMV would be $1,125,000 which is less than the current exemption amount. In this case, the entire IRA would be protected during

---

[2] 11 U.S.C. 522(b)(3)(C), 522(d)(12), 522(n)

[3] 11 U.S.C 104

[4] 75 FR 8747; Also note 11 U.S.C. 522(n) provides for an unspecified increase in such amount "if the interests of justice so require."

[5] 11 U.S.C. 522(a)(2)

bankruptcy via the statutory exemption in the Bankruptcy Code. This area is often overlooked by IRA owners and professional advisors alike.

Case Study – Matthew Files Bankruptcy

Matthew was in the real estate business during the boom times of the mid-2000's. He was very successful and acquired substantial holdings personally and inside his IRA. The IRA holdings consisted mainly of a minority interest in an LP that had other partners. One of the other partners was also the General Partner (GP) of the partnership. The LP primarily bought and held raw land for future development. The property produced no rents or income of any kind.

When the real estate market crashed in the late 2000's, the value of the land held by the LP dropped as if pushed off a cliff. There were several banks involved that had loaned money to the LP. At least one parcel was foreclosed upon and lost to the bank. The LP received a deficiency notice that the bank intended to sue the LP for the remainder of the outstanding loan since the foreclosed parcel did not bring enough at auction to cover the entire debt. Most of the other parcels were threatened with, or in various stages of, foreclosure as well. During this period, the GP was actively negotiating with every possible lending source it could find, including the banks already involved, trying to keep the whole deal together. They negotiated for credit extensions, reductions in interest rates, new terms and anything else possible to avoid losing all the parcels to foreclosure.

During this time, Matthew's other non-IRA deals turned sour also, and it became increasingly obvious that bankruptcy was the only solution. When Matthew created his personal asset inventory to discuss with his bankruptcy attorney, he found that the IRA statement from his custodian reported the IRA value as $1,500,000. One million dollars was the original amount invested in the LP but clearly not the accurate current value. The other $500,000 of reported IRA value was made up of cash and other marketable securities. Thus Matthew's custodian was still reporting the IRA's original investment or cost basis in the LP on the account statement, making his IRA appear much more valuable than it really was.

This caused another problem because at $1,500,000, the IRA had roughly $400,000 of exposure beyond the bankruptcy exemption amount of $1,095,000 in effect at the time. Matthew approached his custodian about getting the reported value reduced to either zero or $1 to reflect the fact the IRA was unlikely to ever receive any return from the LP. They refused unless the GP would sign an affidavit attesting that the IRA's interest was essentially worthless. The GP naturally refused to sign such a statement because it would hurt their negotiating position with possible lenders to be on record stating the LP had no value.

After further discussion with the custodian, it was agreed that a formal appraisal report showing FMV would be accepted in lieu of the GP affidavit. Matthew obtained a qualified appraisal that resulted in the FMV of the IRA's LP interest being reduced to essentially zero. The custodian updated the account statement to reflect the correct valuation which now showed the IRA at $500,000.

Matthew proceeded with the bankruptcy a few months later and was able to properly claim the entire IRA as exempt property under the rules. The key to this case was Matthew addressing the issue well in advance of the actual bankruptcy proceeding. The entire process took a few months before the account value was corrected. This case highlights the importance of proper valuation of IRA assets even in non-tax related matters. It also shows how discounted assets can work to the benefit of the IRA owner and what a key role FMV plays in various scenarios.

State Creditor Protection Rules for IRAs

As mentioned previously, a state-by-state review of creditor protection laws pertaining to IRAs is beyond the scope of this book. However, in general, each state has its own rules as to what assets are exempt from attachment when a person is sued. Lawsuits arising from car accidents, slip and fall situations, other injuries, bad business deals, personal guarantees on loans and others can be financially devastating to the defendant and their family. State law generally protects certain assets in these cases similar to how various assets have statutory protections in bankruptcy proceedings as outlined in the last section.

Some states offer one hundred percent protection for IRAs with no limitation on value. Other states offer very little protection at all. We will use Nevada as an example in our case study. Nevada currently allows an exemption for IRA assets up to $500,000. This is very similar to the federal bankruptcy exemption described earlier but with a lower threshold.

Case Study – Carol is Sued after a Car Accident

Carol was involved in a car accident where she rear-ended the car in front of her which had stopped suddenly. There was significant damage to both vehicles, and the other driver was transported to a hospital by ambulance with neck and back pain.

Shortly after the accident, Carol received notice she was being sued by the other driver for unspecified damages. Both Carol and the other driver were from Nevada and the lawsuit was filed in Nevada.

Carol began a series of meetings with her attorney to prepare for the case. The hope was to reach a settlement and avoid going to court. Part of the process included determining which assets she owned that would be exempt if the case were to proceed to court. Carol had an IRA holding units of a private investment fund (PIF). Her units had a NAV of $750,000 and FMV of $487,500 reflecting a 35% discount based on a qualified appraisal. Carol had been diligent about keeping her custodian updated on the current FMV of the units, and her account statement reflected the correct FMV of $487,500. Since this amount was less than the Nevada statutory exemption of $500,000, Carol's IRA was fully protected in the event they could not reach a settlement and ended up in court.

Both case studies highlight very unfortunate circumstances for those involved. Such circumstances can befall anyone at any time without warning. Fortunately, by following the rules on how to properly report FMV for non-traded assets, both parties were able to maintain their retirement funds to provide for their future financial security.

In both examples, the IRA owners already held the non-traded assets in their accounts prior to the circumstances leading to bankruptcy or creditor issues. They simply followed the required rules to ensure the valuations were correctly reported which luckily resulted in a positive result for them.

IRA Beneficiary Trusts

A method of protecting inherited IRAs from creditors is to name a specialized trust as the benficiary. Such a trust must be properly drafted in order to protect the IRA and maintain the stretch RMD options for the ultimate beneficiary. Using a specialized IRA beneficiary trust as the named beneficiary on an IRA is not specific to accounts holding assets subject to valuation adjustment. They are typically used anytime a large IRA is involved in order to protect the bulk of the account from creditors of the beneficiary because courts have interpreted protections for inherited IRAs differently from state to state.

A detailed discussion of this type of trust and the various court cases involving inherited IRAs is beyond the scope of this text. I strongly encourage you to seek professional counsel to determine if using an IRA beneficiary trust is appropriate for you.

PART FIVE

Conclusion
Appendices
Index
Acknowledgments
About the Author

Conclusion

What Will You Do Now?

Hopefully, this book has opened your eyes to some interesting ideas. The concepts and strategies presented can make a huge financial difference for many families.

Advisors and individuals that fail to plan for the huge pending tax bite on retirement assets are missing a large piece of the planning puzzle. Taxes and inflation are two of the biggest threats to retirement income security. They are also two of the most difficult threats to plan for because their true impact cannot be known with certainty in advance. As outlined in the introduction, Uncle Sam and state governments have a huge stake in retirement accounts and must be paid before the IRA owner can enjoy the fruits of his or her labor. How much tax these government entities will require at various intervals in a person's retirement lifecycle is the subject of much debate.

Luckily, you have read this book and become more informed about strategies to limit the potential damage to your financial future caused by these forces. IRA owners are encouraged to review this information with their professional advisors to determine the best approach for their personal situation. You should also share this information with friends, family members and associates that can benefit from these strategies.

Professional advisors are encouraged to share this information with clients, prospects and other professionals such as key centers of influence and referral sources in their community. Look for opportunities within your existing client base to apply the strategies in this book and help them tackle the tax issues inherent in retirement accounts.

The key is to act now. Opportunities come and go. Laws, regulations and tax rates change. And financial markets can be fickle. Review your situation and make informed decisions about how to use the information contained herein. And let me know about it! Toward the back of the book you'll find ways to connect with me via social media and the internet. I'd love to hear your success stories and perhaps share some of them with others in the community.

Table 1 - Single Life Expectancy

Age	Life Expectancy	Age	Life Expectancy
0	82.4	28	55.3
1	81.6	29	54.3
2	80.6	30	53.3
3	79.7	31	52.4
4	78.7	32	51.4
5	77.7	33	50.4
6	76.7	34	49.4
7	75.8	35	48.5
8	74.8	36	47.5
9	73.8	37	46.5
10	72.8	38	45.6
11	71.8	39	44.6
12	70.8	40	43.6
13	69.9	41	42.7
14	68.9	42	41.7
15	67.9	43	40.7
16	66.9	44	39.8
17	66	45	38.8
18	65	46	37.9
19	64	47	37
20	63	48	36
21	62.1	49	35.1
22	61.1	50	34.2
23	60.1	51	33.3
24	59.1	52	32.3
25	58.2	53	31.4
26	57.2	54	30.5
27	56.2	55	29.6

Table 1 - Single Life Expectancy (continued)

Age	Life Expectancy	Age	Life Expectancy
56	28.7	84	8.1
57	27.9	85	7.6
58	27	86	7.1
59	26.1	87	6.7
60	25.2	88	6.3
61	24.4	89	5.9
62	23.5	90	5.5
63	22.7	91	5.2
64	21.8	92	4.9
65	21	93	4.6
66	20.2	94	4.3
67	19.4	95	4.1
68	18.6	96	3.8
69	17.8	97	3.6
70	17	98	3.4
71	16.3	99	3.1
72	15.5	100	2.9
73	14.8	101	2.7
74	14.1	102	2.5
75	13.4	103	2.3
76	12.7	104	2.1
77	12.1	105	1.9
78	11.4	106	1.7
79	10.8	107	1.5
80	10.2	108	1.4
81	9.7	109	1.2
82	9.1	110	1.1
83	8.6	111 and over	1

Table II - Joint and Last Survivor Expectancy

Ages	20	21	22	23	24	25	26	27	28	29
20	70.1	69.6	69.1	68.7	68.3	67.9	67.5	67.2	66.9	66.6
21	69.6	69.1	68.6	68.2	67.7	67.3	66.9	66.6	66.2	65.9
22	69.1	68.6	68.1	67.6	67.2	66.7	66.3	65.9	65.6	65.2
23	68.7	68.2	67.6	67.1	66.6	66.2	65.7	65.3	64.9	64.6
24	68.3	67.7	67.2	66.6	66.1	65.6	65.2	64.7	64.3	63.9
25	67.9	67.3	66.7	66.2	65.6	65.1	64.6	64.2	63.7	63.3
26	67.5	66.9	66.3	65.7	65.2	64.6	64.1	63.6	63.2	62.8
27	67.2	66.6	65.9	65.3	64.7	64.2	63.6	63.1	62.7	62.2
28	66.9	66.2	65.6	64.9	64.3	63.7	63.2	62.7	62.1	61.7
29	66.6	65.9	65.2	64.6	63.9	63.3	62.8	62.2	61.7	61.2
30	66.3	65.6	64.9	64.2	63.6	62.9	62.3	61.8	61.2	60.7
31	66.1	65.3	64.6	63.9	63.2	62.6	62	61.4	60.8	60.2
32	65.8	65.1	64.3	63.6	62.9	62.2	61.6	61	60.4	59.8
33	65.6	64.8	64.1	63.3	62.6	61.9	61.3	60.6	60	59.4
34	65.4	64.6	63.8	63.1	62.3	61.6	60.9	60.3	59.6	59
35	65.2	64.4	63.6	62.8	62.1	61.4	60.6	59.9	59.3	58.6
36	65	64.2	63.4	62.6	61.9	61.1	60.4	59.6	59	58.3
37	64.9	64	63.2	62.4	61.6	60.9	60.1	59.4	58.7	58
38	64.7	63.9	63	62.2	61.4	60.6	59.9	59.1	58.4	57.7
39	64.6	63.7	62.9	62.1	61.2	60.4	59.6	58.9	58.1	57.4
40	64.4	63.6	62.7	61.9	61.1	60.2	59.4	58.7	57.9	57.1
41	64.3	63.5	62.6	61.7	60.9	60.1	59.3	58.5	57.7	56.9
42	64.2	63.3	62.5	61.6	60.8	59.9	59.1	58.3	57.5	56.7
43	64.1	63.2	62.4	61.5	60.6	59.8	58.9	58.1	57.3	56.5
44	64	63.1	62.2	61.4	60.5	59.6	58.8	57.9	57.1	56.3
45	64	63	62.2	61.3	60.4	59.5	58.6	57.8	56.9	56.1
46	63.9	63	62.1	61.2	60.3	59.4	58.5	57.7	56.8	56
47	63.8	62.9	62	61.1	60.2	59.3	58.4	57.5	56.7	55.8
48	63.7	62.8	61.9	61	60.1	59.2	58.3	57.4	56.5	55.7
49	63.7	62.8	61.8	60.9	60	59.1	58.2	57.3	56.4	55.6
50	63.6	62.7	61.8	60.8	59.9	59	58.1	57.2	56.3	55.4

Table II - Joint and Last Survivor Expectancy (cont.)

Ages	20	21	22	23	24	25	26	27	28	29
51	63.6	62.6	61.7	60.8	59.9	58.9	58	57.1	56.2	55.3
52	63.5	62.6	61.7	60.7	59.8	58.9	58	57.1	56.1	55.2
53	63.5	62.5	61.6	60.7	59.7	58.8	57.9	57	56.1	55.2
54	63.5	62.5	61.6	60.6	59.7	58.8	57.8	56.9	56	55.1
55	63.4	62.5	61.5	60.6	59.6	58.7	57.8	56.8	55.9	55
56	63.4	62.4	61.5	60.5	59.6	58.7	57.7	56.8	55.9	54.9
57	63.4	62.4	61.5	60.5	59.6	58.6	57.7	56.7	55.8	54.9
58	63.3	62.4	61.4	60.5	59.5	58.6	57.6	56.7	55.8	54.8
59	63.3	62.3	61.4	60.4	59.5	58.5	57.6	56.7	55.7	54.8
60	63.3	62.3	61.4	60.4	59.5	58.5	57.6	56.6	55.7	54.7
61	63.3	62.3	61.3	60.4	59.4	58.5	57.5	56.6	55.6	54.7
62	63.2	62.3	61.3	60.4	59.4	58.4	57.5	56.5	55.6	54.7
63	63.2	62.3	61.3	60.3	59.4	58.4	57.5	56.5	55.6	54.6
64	63.2	62.2	61.3	60.3	59.4	58.4	57.4	56.5	55.5	54.6
65	63.2	62.2	61.3	60.3	59.3	58.4	57.4	56.5	55.5	54.6
66	63.2	62.2	61.2	60.3	59.3	58.4	57.4	56.4	55.5	54.5
67	63.2	62.2	61.2	60.3	59.3	58.3	57.4	56.4	55.5	54.5
68	63.1	62.2	61.2	60.2	59.3	58.3	57.4	56.4	55.4	54.5
69	63.1	62.2	61.2	60.2	59.3	58.3	57.3	56.4	55.4	54.5
70	63.1	62.2	61.2	60.2	59.3	58.3	57.3	56.4	55.4	54.4
71	63.1	62.1	61.2	60.2	59.2	58.3	57.3	56.4	55.4	54.4
72	63.1	62.1	61.2	60.2	59.2	58.3	57.3	56.3	55.4	54.4
73	63.1	62.1	61.2	60.2	59.2	58.3	57.3	56.3	55.4	54.4
74	63.1	62.1	61.2	60.2	59.2	58.2	57.3	56.3	55.4	54.4
75	63.1	62.1	61.1	60.2	59.2	58.2	57.3	56.3	55.3	54.4
76	63.1	62.1	61.1	60.2	59.2	58.2	57.3	56.3	55.3	54.4
77	63.1	62.1	61.1	60.2	59.2	58.2	57.3	56.3	55.3	54.4
78	63.1	62.1	61.1	60.2	59.2	58.2	57.3	56.3	55.3	54.4
79	63.1	62.1	61.1	60.2	59.2	58.2	57.2	56.3	55.3	54.3
80	63.1	62.1	61.1	60.1	59.2	58.2	57.2	56.3	55.3	54.3
81	63.1	62.1	61.1	60.1	59.2	58.2	57.2	56.3	55.3	54.3
82	63.1	62.1	61.1	60.1	59.2	58.2	57.2	56.3	55.3	54.3
83	63.1	62.1	61.1	60.1	59.2	58.2	57.2	56.3	55.3	54.3
84	63	62.1	61.1	60.1	59.2	58.2	57.2	56.3	55.3	54.3

Table II - Joint and Last Survivor Expectancy (cont.)

Ages	20	21	22	23	24	25	26	27	28	29
85	63	62.1	61.1	60.1	59.2	58.2	57.2	56.3	55.3	54.3
86	63	62.1	61.1	60.1	59.2	58.2	57.2	56.2	55.3	54.3
87	63	62.1	61.1	60.1	59.2	58.2	57.2	56.2	55.3	54.3
88	63	62.1	61.1	60.1	59.2	58.2	57.2	56.2	55.3	54.3
89	63	62.1	61.1	60.1	59.1	58.2	57.2	56.2	55.3	54.3
90	63	62.1	61.1	60.1	59.1	58.2	57.2	56.2	55.3	54.3
91	63	62.1	61.1	60.1	59.1	58.2	57.2	56.2	55.3	54.3
92	63	62.1	61.1	60.1	59.1	58.2	57.2	56.2	55.3	54.3
93	63	62.1	61.1	60.1	59.1	58.2	57.2	56.2	55.3	54.3
94	63	62.1	61.1	60.1	59.1	58.2	57.2	56.2	55.3	54.3
95	63	62.1	61.1	60.1	59.1	58.2	57.2	56.2	55.3	54.3
96	63	62.1	61.1	60.1	59.1	58.2	57.2	56.2	55.3	54.3
97	63	62.1	61.1	60.1	59.1	58.2	57.2	56.2	55.3	54.3
98	63	62.1	61.1	60.1	59.1	58.2	57.2	56.2	55.3	54.3
99	63	62.1	61.1	60.1	59.1	58.2	57.2	56.2	55.3	54.3
100	63	62.1	61.1	60.1	59.1	58.2	57.2	56.2	55.3	54.3
101	63	62.1	61.1	60.1	59.1	58.2	57.2	56.2	55.3	54.3
102	63	62.1	61.1	60.1	59.1	58.2	57.2	56.2	55.3	54.3
103	63	62.1	61.1	60.1	59.1	58.2	57.2	56.2	55.3	54.3
104	63	62.1	61.1	60.1	59.1	58.2	57.2	56.2	55.3	54.3
105	63	62.1	61.1	60.1	59.1	58.2	57.2	56.2	55.3	54.3
106	63	62.1	61.1	60.1	59.1	58.2	57.2	56.2	55.3	54.3
107	63	62.1	61.1	60.1	59.1	58.2	57.2	56.2	55.3	54.3
108	63	62.1	61.1	60.1	59.1	58.2	57.2	56.2	55.3	54.3
109	63	62.1	61.1	60.1	59.1	58.2	57.2	56.2	55.3	54.3
110	63	62.1	61.1	60.1	59.1	58.2	57.2	56.2	55.3	54.3
111	63	62.1	61.1	60.1	59.1	58.2	57.2	56.2	55.3	54.3
112	63	62.1	61.1	60.1	59.1	58.2	57.2	56.2	55.3	54.3
113	63	62.1	61.1	60.1	59.1	58.2	57.2	56.2	55.3	54.3
114	63	62.1	61.1	60.1	59.1	58.2	57.2	56.2	55.3	54.3
115+	63	62.1	61.1	60.1	59.1	58.2	57.2	56.2	55.3	54.3

Table II - Joint and Last Survivor Expectancy (cont.)

Ages	30	31	32	33	34	35	36	37	38	39
30	60.2	59.7	59.2	58.8	58.4	58	57.6	57.3	57	56.7
31	59.7	59.2	58.7	58.2	57.8	57.4	57	56.6	56.3	56
32	59.2	58.7	58.2	57.7	57.2	56.8	56.4	56	55.6	55.3
33	58.8	58.2	57.7	57.2	56.7	56.2	55.8	55.4	55	54.7
34	58.4	57.8	57.2	56.7	56.2	55.7	55.3	54.8	54.4	54
35	58	57.4	56.8	56.2	55.7	55.2	54.7	54.3	53.8	53.4
36	57.6	57	56.4	55.8	55.3	54.7	54.2	53.7	53.3	52.8
37	57.3	56.6	56	55.4	54.8	54.3	53.7	53.2	52.7	52.3
38	57	56.3	55.6	55	54.4	53.8	53.3	52.7	52.2	51.7
39	56.7	56	55.3	54.7	54	53.4	52.8	52.3	51.7	51.2
40	56.4	55.7	55	54.3	53.7	53	52.4	51.8	51.3	50.8
41	56.1	55.4	54.7	54	53.3	52.7	52	51.4	50.9	50.3
42	55.9	55.2	54.4	53.7	53	52.3	51.7	51.1	50.4	49.9
43	55.7	54.9	54.2	53.4	52.7	52	51.3	50.7	50.1	49.5
44	55.5	54.7	53.9	53.2	52.4	51.7	51	50.4	49.7	49.1
45	55.3	54.5	53.7	52.9	52.2	51.5	50.7	50	49.4	48.7
46	55.1	54.3	53.5	52.7	52	51.2	50.5	49.8	49.1	48.4
47	55	54.1	53.3	52.5	51.7	51	50.2	49.5	48.8	48.1
48	54.8	54	53.2	52.3	51.5	50.8	50	49.2	48.5	47.8
49	54.7	53.8	53	52.2	51.4	50.6	49.8	49	48.2	47.5
50	54.6	53.7	52.9	52	51.2	50.4	49.6	48.8	48	47.3
51	54.5	53.6	52.7	51.9	51	50.2	49.4	48.6	47.8	47
52	54.4	53.5	52.6	51.7	50.9	50	49.2	48.4	47.6	46.8
53	54.3	53.4	52.5	51.6	50.8	49.9	49.1	48.2	47.4	46.6
54	54.2	53.3	52.4	51.5	50.6	49.8	48.9	48.1	47.2	46.4
55	54.1	53.2	52.3	51.4	50.5	49.7	48.8	47.9	47.1	46.3
56	54	53.1	52.2	51.3	50.4	49.5	48.7	47.8	47	46.1
57	54	53	52.1	51.2	50.3	49.4	48.6	47.7	46.8	46
58	53.9	53	52.1	51.2	50.3	49.4	48.5	47.6	46.7	45.8
59	53.8	52.9	52	51.1	50.2	49.3	48.4	47.5	46.6	45.7
60	53.8	52.9	51.9	51	50.1	49.2	48.3	47.4	46.5	45.6

Table II - Joint and Last Survivor Expectancy (cont.)

Ages	30	31	32	33	34	35	36	37	38	39
95	53.3	52.4	51.4	50.4	49.5	48.5	47.5	46.5	45.6	44.6
96	53.3	52.4	51.4	50.4	49.5	48.5	47.5	46.5	45.6	44.6
97	53.3	52.4	51.4	50.4	49.5	48.5	47.5	46.5	45.6	44.6
98	53.3	52.4	51.4	50.4	49.5	48.5	47.5	46.5	45.6	44.6
99	53.3	52.4	51.4	50.4	49.5	48.5	47.5	46.5	45.6	44.6
100	53.3	52.4	51.4	50.4	49.5	48.5	47.5	46.5	45.6	44.6
101	53.3	52.4	51.4	50.4	49.5	48.5	47.5	46.5	45.6	44.6
102	53.3	52.4	51.4	50.4	49.5	48.5	47.5	46.5	45.6	44.6
103	53.3	52.4	51.4	50.4	49.5	48.5	47.5	46.5	45.6	44.6
104	53.3	52.4	51.4	50.4	49.5	48.5	47.5	46.5	45.6	44.6
105	53.3	52.4	51.4	50.4	49.4	48.5	47.5	46.5	45.6	44.6
106	53.3	52.4	51.4	50.4	49.4	48.5	47.5	46.5	45.6	44.6
107	53.3	52.4	51.4	50.4	49.4	48.5	47.5	46.5	45.6	44.6
108	53.3	52.4	51.4	50.4	49.4	48.5	47.5	46.5	45.6	44.6
109	53.3	52.4	51.4	50.4	49.4	48.5	47.5	46.5	45.6	44.6
110	53.3	52.4	51.4	50.4	49.4	48.5	47.5	46.5	45.6	44.6
111	53.3	52.4	51.4	50.4	49.4	48.5	47.5	46.5	45.6	44.6
112	53.3	52.4	51.4	50.4	49.4	48.5	47.5	46.5	45.6	44.6
113	53.3	52.4	51.4	50.4	49.4	48.5	47.5	46.5	45.6	44.6
114	53.3	52.4	51.4	50.4	49.4	48.5	47.5	46.5	45.6	44.6
115+	53.3	52.4	51.4	50.4	49.4	48.5	47.5	46.5	45.6	44.6

Ages	40	41	42	43	44	45	46	47	48	49
40	50.2	49.8	49.3	48.9	48.5	48.1	47.7	47.4	47.1	46.8
41	49.8	49.3	48.8	48.3	47.9	47.5	47.1	46.7	46.4	46.1
42	49.3	48.8	48.3	47.8	47.3	46.9	46.5	46.1	45.8	45.4
43	48.9	48.3	47.8	47.3	46.8	46.3	45.9	45.5	45.1	44.8
44	48.5	47.9	47.3	46.8	46.3	45.8	45.4	44.9	44.5	44.2
45	48.1	47.5	46.9	46.3	45.8	45.3	44.8	44.4	44	43.6
46	47.7	47.1	46.5	45.9	45.4	44.8	44.3	43.9	43.4	43
47	47.4	46.7	46.1	45.5	44.9	44.4	43.9	43.4	42.9	42.4
48	47.1	46.4	45.8	45.1	44.5	44	43.4	42.9	42.4	41.9

Table II - Joint and Last Survivor Expectancy (cont.)

Ages	40	41	42	43	44	45	46	47	48	49
49	46.8	46.1	45.4	44.8	44.2	43.6	43	42.4	41.9	41.4
50	46.5	45.8	45.1	44.4	43.8	43.2	42.6	42	41.5	40.9
51	46.3	45.5	44.8	44.1	43.5	42.8	42.2	41.6	41	40.5
52	46	45.3	44.6	43.8	43.2	42.5	41.8	41.2	40.6	40.1
53	45.8	45.1	44.3	43.6	42.9	42.2	41.5	40.9	40.3	39.7
54	45.6	44.8	44.1	43.3	42.6	41.9	41.2	40.5	39.9	39.3
55	45.5	44.7	43.9	43.1	42.4	41.6	40.9	40.2	39.6	38.9
56	45.3	44.5	43.7	42.9	42.1	41.4	40.7	40	39.3	38.6
57	45.1	44.3	43.5	42.7	41.9	41.2	40.4	39.7	39	38.3
58	45	44.2	43.3	42.5	41.7	40.9	40.2	39.4	38.7	38
59	44.9	44	43.2	42.4	41.5	40.7	40	39.2	38.5	37.8
60	44.7	43.9	43	42.2	41.4	40.6	39.8	39	38.2	37.5
61	44.6	43.8	42.9	42.1	41.2	40.4	39.6	38.8	38	37.3
62	44.5	43.7	42.8	41.9	41.1	40.3	39.4	38.6	37.8	37.1
63	44.5	43.6	42.7	41.8	41	40.1	39.3	38.5	37.7	36.9
64	44.4	43.5	42.6	41.7	40.8	40	39.2	38.3	37.5	36.7
65	44.3	43.4	42.5	41.6	40.7	39.9	39	38.2	37.4	36.6
66	44.2	43.3	42.4	41.5	40.6	39.8	38.9	38.1	37.2	36.4
67	44.2	43.3	42.3	41.4	40.6	39.7	38.8	38	37.1	36.3
68	44.1	43.2	42.3	41.4	40.5	39.6	38.7	37.9	37	36.2
69	44.1	43.1	42.2	41.3	40.4	39.5	38.6	37.8	36.9	36
70	44	43.1	42.2	41.3	40.3	39.4	38.6	37.7	36.8	35.9
71	44	43	42.1	41.2	40.3	39.4	38.5	37.6	36.7	35.9
72	43.9	43	42.1	41.1	40.2	39.3	38.4	37.5	36.6	35.8
73	43.9	43	42	41.1	40.2	39.3	38.4	37.5	36.6	35.7
74	43.9	42.9	42	41.1	40.1	39.2	38.3	37.4	36.5	35.6
75	43.8	42.9	42	41	40.1	39.2	38.3	37.4	36.5	35.6
76	43.8	42.9	41.9	41	40.1	39.1	38.2	37.3	36.4	35.5
77	43.8	42.9	41.9	41	40	39.1	38.2	37.3	36.4	35.5
78	43.8	42.8	41.9	40.9	40	39.1	38.2	37.2	36.3	35.4
79	43.8	42.8	41.9	40.9	40	39.1	38.1	37.2	36.3	35.4
80	43.7	42.8	41.8	40.9	40	39	38.1	37.2	36.3	35.4
81	43.7	42.8	41.8	40.9	39.9	39	38.1	37.2	36.2	35.3
82	43.7	42.8	41.8	40.9	39.9	39	38.1	37.1	36.2	35.3

Table II - Joint and Last Survivor Expectancy (cont.)

Ages	40	41	42	43	44	45	46	47	48	49
83	43.7	42.8	41.8	40.9	39.9	39	38	37.1	36.2	35.3
84	43.7	42.7	41.8	40.8	39.9	39	38	37.1	36.2	35.3
85	43.7	42.7	41.8	40.8	39.9	38.9	38	37.1	36.2	35.2
86	43.7	42.7	41.8	40.8	39.9	38.9	38	37.1	36.1	35.2
87	43.7	42.7	41.8	40.8	39.9	38.9	38	37	36.1	35.2
88	43.7	42.7	41.8	40.8	39.9	38.9	38	37	36.1	35.2
89	43.7	42.7	41.7	40.8	39.8	38.9	38	37	36.1	35.2
90	43.7	42.7	41.7	40.8	39.8	38.9	38	37	36.1	35.2
91	43.7	42.7	41.7	40.8	39.8	38.9	37.9	37	36.1	35.2
92	43.7	42.7	41.7	40.8	39.8	38.9	37.9	37	36.1	35.1
93	43.7	42.7	41.7	40.8	39.8	38.9	37.9	37	36.1	35.1
94	43.7	42.7	41.7	40.8	39.8	38.9	37.9	37	36.1	35.1
95	43.6	42.7	41.7	40.8	39.8	38.9	37.9	37	36.1	35.1
96	43.6	42.7	41.7	40.8	39.8	38.9	37.9	37	36.1	35.1
97	43.6	42.7	41.7	40.8	39.8	38.9	37.9	37	36.1	35.1
98	43.6	42.7	41.7	40.8	39.8	38.9	37.9	37	36	35.1
99	43.6	42.7	41.7	40.8	39.8	38.9	37.9	37	36	35.1
100	43.6	42.7	41.7	40.8	39.8	38.9	37.9	37	36	35.1
101	43.6	42.7	41.7	40.8	39.8	38.9	37.9	37	36	35.1
102	43.6	42.7	41.7	40.8	39.8	38.9	37.9	37	36	35.1
103	43.6	42.7	41.7	40.8	39.8	38.9	37.9	37	36	35.1
104	43.6	42.7	41.7	40.8	39.8	38.8	37.9	37	36	35.1
105	43.6	42.7	41.7	40.8	39.8	38.8	37.9	37	36	35.1
106	43.6	42.7	41.7	40.8	39.8	38.8	37.9	37	36	35.1
107	43.6	42.7	41.7	40.8	39.8	38.8	37.9	37	36	35.1
108	43.6	42.7	41.7	40.8	39.8	38.8	37.9	37	36	35.1
109	43.6	42.7	41.7	40.7	39.8	38.8	37.9	37	36	35.1
110	43.6	42.7	41.7	40.7	39.8	38.8	37.9	37	36	35.1
111	43.6	42.7	41.7	40.7	39.8	38.8	37.9	37	36	35.1
112	43.6	42.7	41.7	40.7	39.8	38.8	37.9	37	36	35.1
113	43.6	42.7	41.7	40.7	39.8	38.8	37.9	37	36	35.1
114	43.6	42.7	41.7	40.7	39.8	38.8	37.9	37	36	35.1
115+	43.6	42.7	41.7	40.7	39.8	38.8	37.9	37	36	35.1

Table II - Joint and Last Survivor Expectancy (cont.)

Ages	50	51	52	53	54	55	56	57	58	59
50	40.4	40	39.5	39.1	38.7	38.3	38	37.6	37.3	37.1
51	40	39.5	39	38.5	38.1	37.7	37.4	37	36.7	36.4
52	39.5	39	38.5	38	37.6	37.2	36.8	36.4	36	35.7
53	39.1	38.5	38	37.5	37.1	36.6	36.2	35.8	35.4	35.1
54	38.7	38.1	37.6	37.1	36.6	36.1	35.7	35.2	34.8	34.5
55	38.3	37.7	37.2	36.6	36.1	35.6	35.1	34.7	34.3	33.9
56	38	37.4	36.8	36.2	35.7	35.1	34.7	34.2	33.7	33.3
57	37.6	37	36.4	35.8	35.2	34.7	34.2	33.7	33.2	32.8
58	37.3	36.7	36	35.4	34.8	34.3	33.7	33.2	32.8	32.3
59	37.1	36.4	35.7	35.1	34.5	33.9	33.3	32.8	32.3	31.8
60	36.8	36.1	35.4	34.8	34.1	33.5	32.9	32.4	31.9	31.3
61	36.6	35.8	35.1	34.5	33.8	33.2	32.6	32	31.4	30.9
62	36.3	35.6	34.9	34.2	33.5	32.9	32.2	31.6	31.1	30.5
63	36.1	35.4	34.6	33.9	33.2	32.6	31.9	31.3	30.7	30.1
64	35.9	35.2	34.4	33.7	33	32.3	31.6	31	30.4	29.8
65	35.8	35	34.2	33.5	32.7	32	31.4	30.7	30	29.4
66	35.6	34.8	34	33.3	32.5	31.8	31.1	30.4	29.8	29.1
67	35.5	34.7	33.9	33.1	32.3	31.6	30.9	30.2	29.5	28.8
68	35.3	34.5	33.7	32.9	32.1	31.4	30.7	29.9	29.2	28.6
69	35.2	34.4	33.6	32.8	32	31.2	30.5	29.7	29	28.3
70	35.1	34.3	33.4	32.6	31.8	31.1	30.3	29.5	28.8	28.1
71	35	34.2	33.3	32.5	31.7	30.9	30.1	29.4	28.6	27.9
72	34.9	34.1	33.2	32.4	31.6	30.8	30	29.2	28.4	27.7
73	34.8	34	33.1	32.3	31.5	30.6	29.8	29.1	28.3	27.5
74	34.8	33.9	33	32.2	31.4	30.5	29.7	28.9	28.1	27.4
75	34.7	33.8	33	32.1	31.3	30.4	29.6	28.8	28	27.2
76	34.6	33.8	32.9	32	31.2	30.3	29.5	28.7	27.9	27.1
77	34.6	33.7	32.8	32	31.1	30.3	29.4	28.6	27.8	27
78	34.5	33.6	32.8	31.9	31	30.2	29.3	28.5	27.7	26.9
79	34.5	33.6	32.7	31.8	31	30.1	29.3	28.4	27.6	26.8
80	34.5	33.6	32.7	31.8	30.9	30.1	29.2	28.4	27.5	26.7
81	34.4	33.5	32.6	31.8	30.9	30	29.2	28.3	27.5	26.6
82	34.4	33.5	32.6	31.7	30.8	30	29.1	28.3	27.4	26.6
83	34.4	33.5	32.6	31.7	30.8	29.9	29.1	28.2	27.4	26.5

Table II - Joint and Last Survivor Expectancy (cont.)

Ages	50	51	52	53	54	55	56	57	58	59
84	34.3	33.4	32.5	31.7	30.8	29.9	29	28.2	27.3	26.5
85	34.3	33.4	32.5	31.6	30.7	29.9	29	28.1	27.3	26.4
86	34.3	33.4	32.5	31.6	30.7	29.8	29	28.1	27.2	26.4
87	34.3	33.4	32.5	31.6	30.7	29.8	28.9	28.1	27.2	26.4
88	34.3	33.4	32.5	31.6	30.7	29.8	28.9	28	27.2	26.3
89	34.3	33.3	32.4	31.5	30.7	29.8	28.9	28	27.2	26.3
90	34.2	33.3	32.4	31.5	30.6	29.8	28.9	28	27.1	26.3
91	34.2	33.3	32.4	31.5	30.6	29.7	28.9	28	27.1	26.3
92	34.2	33.3	32.4	31.5	30.6	29.7	28.8	28	27.1	26.2
93	34.2	33.3	32.4	31.5	30.6	29.7	28.8	28	27.1	26.2
94	34.2	33.3	32.4	31.5	30.6	29.7	28.8	27.9	27.1	26.2
95	34.2	33.3	32.4	31.5	30.6	29.7	28.8	27.9	27.1	26.2
96	34.2	33.3	32.4	31.5	30.6	29.7	28.8	27.9	27	26.2
97	34.2	33.3	32.4	31.5	30.6	29.7	28.8	27.9	27	26.2
98	34.2	33.3	32.4	31.5	30.6	29.7	28.8	27.9	27	26.2
99	34.2	33.3	32.4	31.5	30.6	29.7	28.8	27.9	27	26.2
100	34.2	33.3	32.4	31.5	30.6	29.7	28.8	27.9	27	26.1
101	34.2	33.3	32.4	31.5	30.6	29.7	28.8	27.9	27	26.1
102	34.2	33.3	32.4	31.4	30.5	29.7	28.8	27.9	27	26.1
103	34.2	33.3	32.4	31.4	30.5	29.7	28.8	27.9	27	26.1
104	34.2	33.3	32.4	31.4	30.5	29.6	28.8	27.9	27	26.1
105	34.2	33.3	32.3	31.4	30.5	29.6	28.8	27.9	27	26.1
106	34.2	33.3	32.3	31.4	30.5	29.6	28.8	27.9	27	26.1
107	34.2	33.3	32.3	31.4	30.5	29.6	28.8	27.9	27	26.1
108	34.2	33.3	32.3	31.4	30.5	29.6	28.8	27.9	27	26.1
109	34.2	33.3	32.3	31.4	30.5	29.6	28.7	27.9	27	26.1
110	34.2	33.3	32.3	31.4	30.5	29.6	28.7	27.9	27	26.1
111	34.2	33.3	32.3	31.4	30.5	29.6	28.7	27.9	27	26.1
112	34.2	33.3	32.3	31.4	30.5	29.6	28.7	27.9	27	26.1
113	34.2	33.3	32.3	31.4	30.5	29.6	28.7	27.9	27	26.1
114	34.2	33.3	32.3	31.4	30.5	29.6	28.7	27.9	27	26.1

Table II - Joint and Last Survivor Expectancy (cont.)

Ages	60	61	62	63	64	65	66	67	68	69
60	30.9	30.4	30	29.6	29.2	28.8	28.5	28.2	27.9	27.6
61	30.4	29.9	29.5	29	28.6	28.3	27.9	27.6	27.3	27
62	30	29.5	29	28.5	28.1	27.7	27.3	27	26.7	26.4
63	29.6	29	28.5	28.1	27.6	27.2	26.8	26.4	26.1	25.7
64	29.2	28.6	28.1	27.6	27.1	26.7	26.3	25.9	25.5	25.2
65	28.8	28.3	27.7	27.2	26.7	26.2	25.8	25.4	25	24.6
66	28.5	27.9	27.3	26.8	26.3	25.8	25.3	24.9	24.5	24.1
67	28.2	27.6	27	26.4	25.9	25.4	24.9	24.4	24	23.6
68	27.9	27.3	26.7	26.1	25.5	25	24.5	24	23.5	23.1
69	27.6	27	26.4	25.7	25.2	24.6	24.1	23.6	23.1	22.6
70	27.4	26.7	26.1	25.4	24.8	24.3	23.7	23.2	22.7	22.2
71	27.2	26.5	25.8	25.2	24.5	23.9	23.4	22.8	22.3	21.8
72	27	26.3	25.6	24.9	24.3	23.7	23.1	22.5	22	21.4
73	26.8	26.1	25.4	24.7	24	23.4	22.8	22.2	21.6	21.1
74	26.6	25.9	25.2	24.5	23.8	23.1	22.5	21.9	21.3	20.8
75	26.5	25.7	25	24.3	23.6	22.9	22.3	21.6	21	20.5
76	26.3	25.6	24.8	24.1	23.4	22.7	22	21.4	20.8	20.2
77	26.2	25.4	24.7	23.9	23.2	22.5	21.8	21.2	20.6	19.9
78	26.1	25.3	24.6	23.8	23.1	22.4	21.7	21	20.3	19.7
79	26	25.2	24.4	23.7	22.9	22.2	21.5	20.8	20.1	19.5
80	25.9	25.1	24.3	23.6	22.8	22.1	21.3	20.6	20	19.3
81	25.8	25	24.2	23.4	22.7	21.9	21.2	20.5	19.8	19.1
82	25.8	24.9	24.1	23.4	22.6	21.8	21.1	20.4	19.7	19
83	25.7	24.9	24.1	23.3	22.5	21.7	21	20.2	19.5	18.8
84	25.6	24.8	24	23.2	22.4	21.6	20.9	20.1	19.4	18.7
85	25.6	24.8	23.9	23.1	22.3	21.6	20.8	20.1	19.3	18.6
86	25.5	24.7	23.9	23.1	22.3	21.5	20.7	20	19.2	18.5
87	25.5	24.7	23.8	23	22.2	21.4	20.7	19.9	19.2	18.4
88	25.5	24.6	23.8	23	22.2	21.4	20.6	19.8	19.1	18.3
89	25.4	24.6	23.8	22.9	22.1	21.3	20.5	19.8	19	18.3
90	25.4	24.6	23.7	22.9	22.1	21.3	20.5	19.7	19	18.2
91	25.4	24.5	23.7	22.9	22.1	21.3	20.5	19.7	18.9	18.2
92	25.4	24.5	23.7	22.9	22	21.2	20.4	19.6	18.9	18.1
93	25.4	24.5	23.7	22.8	22	21.2	20.4	19.6	18.8	18.1

Table II - Joint and Last Survivor Expectancy (cont.)

Ages	60	61	62	63	64	65	66	67	68	69
94	25.3	24.5	23.6	22.8	22	21.2	20.4	19.6	18.8	18
95	25.3	24.5	23.6	22.8	22	21.1	20.3	19.6	18.8	18
96	25.3	24.5	23.6	22.8	21.9	21.1	20.3	19.5	18.8	18
97	25.3	24.5	23.6	22.8	21.9	21.1	20.3	19.5	18.7	18
98	25.3	24.4	23.6	22.8	21.9	21.1	20.3	19.5	18.7	17.9
99	25.3	24.4	23.6	22.7	21.9	21.1	20.3	19.5	18.7	17.9
100	25.3	24.4	23.6	22.7	21.9	21.1	20.3	19.5	18.7	17.9
101	25.3	24.4	23.6	22.7	21.9	21.1	20.2	19.4	18.7	17.9
102	25.3	24.4	23.6	22.7	21.9	21.1	20.2	19.4	18.6	17.9
103	25.3	24.4	23.6	22.7	21.9	21	20.2	19.4	18.6	17.9
104	25.3	24.4	23.5	22.7	21.9	21	20.2	19.4	18.6	17.8
105	25.3	24.4	23.5	22.7	21.9	21	20.2	19.4	18.6	17.8
106	25.3	24.4	23.5	22.7	21.9	21	20.2	19.4	18.6	17.8
107	25.2	24.4	23.5	22.7	21.8	21	20.2	19.4	18.6	17.8
108	25.2	24.4	23.5	22.7	21.8	21	20.2	19.4	18.6	17.8
109	25.2	24.4	23.5	22.7	21.8	21	20.2	19.4	18.6	17.8
110	25.2	24.4	23.5	22.7	21.8	21	20.2	19.4	18.6	17.8
111	25.2	24.4	23.5	22.7	21.8	21	20.2	19.4	18.6	17.8
112	25.2	24.4	23.5	22.7	21.8	21	20.2	19.4	18.6	17.8
113	25.2	24.4	23.5	22.7	21.8	21	20.2	19.4	18.6	17.8
114	25.2	24.4	23.5	22.7	21.8	21	20.2	19.4	18.6	17.8
115+	25.2	24.4	23.5	22.7	21.8	21	20.2	19.4	18.6	17.8

Ages	70	71	72	73	74	75	76	77	78	79
70	21.8	21.3	20.9	20.6	20.2	19.9	19.6	19.4	19.1	18.9
71	21.3	20.9	20.5	20.1	19.7	19.4	19.1	18.8	18.5	18.3
72	20.9	20.5	20	19.6	19.3	18.9	18.6	18.3	18	17.7
73	20.6	20.1	19.6	19.2	18.8	18.4	18.1	17.8	17.5	17.2
74	20.2	19.7	19.3	18.8	18.4	18	17.6	17.3	17	16.7
75	19.9	19.4	18.9	18.4	18	17.6	17.2	16.8	16.5	16.2

Table II - Joint and Last Survivor Expectancy (cont.)

Ages	70	71	72	73	74	75	76	77	78	79
76	19.6	19.1	18.6	18.1	17.6	17.2	16.8	16.4	16	15.7
77	19.4	18.8	18.3	17.8	17.3	16.8	16.4	16	15.6	15.3
78	19.1	18.5	18	17.5	17	16.5	16	15.6	15.2	14.9
79	18.9	18.3	17.7	17.2	16.7	16.2	15.7	15.3	14.9	14.5
80	18.7	18.1	17.5	16.9	16.4	15.9	15.4	15	14.5	14.1
81	18.5	17.9	17.3	16.7	16.2	15.6	15.1	14.7	14.2	13.8
82	18.3	17.7	17.1	16.5	15.9	15.4	14.9	14.4	13.9	13.5
83	18.2	17.5	16.9	16.3	15.7	15.2	14.7	14.2	13.7	13.2
84	18	17.4	16.7	16.1	15.5	15	14.4	13.9	13.4	13
85	17.9	17.3	16.6	16	15.4	14.8	14.3	13.7	13.2	12.8
86	17.8	17.1	16.5	15.8	15.2	14.6	14.1	13.5	13	12.5
87	17.7	17	16.4	15.7	15.1	14.5	13.9	13.4	12.9	12.4
88	17.6	16.9	16.3	15.6	15	14.4	13.8	13.2	12.7	12.2
89	17.6	16.9	16.2	15.5	14.9	14.3	13.7	13.1	12.6	12
90	17.5	16.8	16.1	15.4	14.8	14.2	13.6	13	12.4	11.9
91	17.4	16.7	16	15.4	14.7	14.1	13.5	12.9	12.3	11.8
92	17.4	16.7	16	15.3	14.6	14	13.4	12.8	12.2	11.7
93	17.3	16.6	15.9	15.2	14.6	13.9	13.3	12.7	12.1	11.6
94	17.3	16.6	15.9	15.2	14.5	13.9	13.2	12.6	12	11.5
95	17.3	16.5	15.8	15.1	14.5	13.8	13.2	12.6	12	11.4
96	17.2	16.5	15.8	15.1	14.4	13.8	13.1	12.5	11.9	11.3
97	17.2	16.5	15.8	15.1	14.4	13.7	13.1	12.5	11.9	11.3
98	17.2	16.4	15.7	15	14.3	13.7	13	12.4	11.8	11.2
99	17.2	16.4	15.7	15	14.3	13.6	13	12.4	11.8	11.2
100	17.1	16.4	15.7	15	14.3	13.6	12.9	12.3	11.7	11.1
101	17.1	16.4	15.6	14.9	14.2	13.6	12.9	12.3	11.7	11.1
102	17.1	16.4	15.6	14.9	14.2	13.5	12.9	12.2	11.6	11
103	17.1	16.3	15.6	14.9	14.2	13.5	12.9	12.2	11.6	11
104	17.1	16.3	15.6	14.9	14.2	13.5	12.8	12.2	11.6	11
105	17.1	16.3	15.6	14.9	14.2	13.5	12.8	12.2	11.5	10.9
106	17.1	16.3	15.6	14.8	14.1	13.5	12.8	12.2	11.5	10.9
107	17	16.3	15.6	14.8	14.1	13.4	12.8	12.1	11.5	10.9
108	17	16.3	15.5	14.8	14.1	13.4	12.8	12.1	11.5	10.9
109	17	16.3	15.5	14.8	14.1	13.4	12.8	12.1	11.5	10.9

Table II - Joint and Last Survivor Expectancy (cont.)

Ages	70	71	72	73	74	75	76	77	78	79
110	17	16.3	15.5	14.8	14.1	13.4	12.7	12.1	11.5	10.9
111	17	16.3	15.5	14.8	14.1	13.4	12.7	12.1	11.5	10.8
112	17	16.3	15.5	14.8	14.1	13.4	12.7	12.1	11.5	10.8
113	17	16.3	15.5	14.8	14.1	13.4	12.7	12.1	11.4	10.8
114	17	16.3	15.5	14.8	14.1	13.4	12.7	12.1	11.4	10.8
115+	17	16.3	15.5	14.8	14.1	13.4	12.7	12.1	11.4	10.8

Ages	80	81	82	83	84	85	86	87	88	89
80	13.8	13.4	13.1	12.8	12.6	12.3	12.1	11.9	11.7	11.5
81	13.4	13.1	12.7	12.4	12.2	11.9	11.7	11.4	11.3	11.1
82	13.1	12.7	12.4	12.1	11.8	11.5	11.3	11	10.8	10.6
83	12.8	12.4	12.1	11.7	11.4	11.1	10.9	10.6	10.4	10.2
84	12.6	12.2	11.8	11.4	11.1	10.8	10.5	10.3	10.1	9.9
85	12.3	11.9	11.5	11.1	10.8	10.5	10.2	9.9	9.7	9.5
86	12.1	11.7	11.3	10.9	10.5	10.2	9.9	9.6	9.4	9.2
87	11.9	11.4	11	10.6	10.3	9.9	9.6	9.4	9.1	8.9
88	11.7	11.3	10.8	10.4	10.1	9.7	9.4	9.1	8.8	8.6
89	11.5	11.1	10.6	10.2	9.9	9.5	9.2	8.9	8.6	8.3
90	11.4	10.9	10.5	10.1	9.7	9.3	9	8.6	8.3	8.1
91	11.3	10.8	10.3	9.9	9.5	9.1	8.8	8.4	8.1	7.9
92	11.2	10.7	10.2	9.8	9.3	9	8.6	8.3	8	7.7
93	11.1	10.6	10.1	9.6	9.2	8.8	8.5	8.1	7.8	7.5
94	11	10.5	10	9.5	9.1	8.7	8.3	8	7.6	7.3
95	10.9	10.4	9.9	9.4	9	8.6	8.2	7.8	7.5	7.2
96	10.8	10.3	9.8	9.3	8.9	8.5	8.1	7.7	7.4	7.1
97	10.7	10.2	9.7	9.2	8.8	8.4	8	7.6	7.3	6.9
98	10.7	10.1	9.6	9.2	8.7	8.3	7.9	7.5	7.1	6.8
99	10.6	10.1	9.6	9.1	8.6	8.2	7.8	7.4	7	6.7
100	10.6	10	9.5	9	8.5	8.1	7.7	7.3	6.9	6.6

Table II - Joint and Last Survivor Expectancy (cont.)

Ages	80	81	82	83	84	85	86	87	88	89
101	10.5	10	9.4	9	8.5	8	7.6	7.2	6.9	6.5
102	10.5	9.9	9.4	8.9	8.4	8	7.5	7.1	6.8	6.4
103	10.4	9.9	9.4	8.8	8.4	7.9	7.5	7.1	6.7	6.3
104	10.4	9.8	9.3	8.8	8.3	7.9	7.4	7	6.6	6.3
105	10.4	9.8	9.3	8.8	8.3	7.8	7.4	7	6.6	6.2
106	10.3	9.8	9.2	8.7	8.2	7.8	7.3	6.9	6.5	6.2
107	10.3	9.8	9.2	8.7	8.2	7.7	7.3	6.9	6.5	6.1
108	10.3	9.7	9.2	8.7	8.2	7.7	7.3	6.8	6.4	6.1
109	10.3	9.7	9.2	8.7	8.2	7.7	7.2	6.8	6.4	6
110	10.3	9.7	9.2	8.6	8.1	7.7	7.2	6.8	6.4	6
111	10.3	9.7	9.1	8.6	8.1	7.6	7.2	6.8	6.3	6
112	10.2	9.7	9.1	8.6	8.1	7.6	7.2	6.7	6.3	5.9
113	10.2	9.7	9.1	8.6	8.1	7.6	7.2	6.7	6.3	5.9
114	10.2	9.7	9.1	8.6	8.1	7.6	7.1	6.7	6.3	5.9
115+	10.2	9.7	9.1	8.6	8.1	7.6	7.1	6.7	6.3	5.9

Ages	90	91	92	93	94	95	96	97	98	99
90	7.8	7.6	7.4	7.2	7.1	6.9	6.8	6.6	6.5	6.4
91	7.6	7.4	7.2	7	6.8	6.7	6.5	6.4	6.3	6.1
92	7.4	7.2	7	6.8	6.6	6.4	6.3	6.1	6	5.9
93	7.2	7	6.8	6.6	6.4	6.2	6.1	5.9	5.8	5.6
94	7.1	6.8	6.6	6.4	6.2	6	5.9	5.7	5.6	5.4
95	6.9	6.7	6.4	6.2	6	5.8	5.7	5.5	5.4	5.2
96	6.8	6.5	6.3	6.1	5.9	5.7	5.5	5.3	5.2	5
97	6.6	6.4	6.1	5.9	5.7	5.5	5.3	5.2	5	4.9
98	6.5	6.3	6	5.8	5.6	5.4	5.2	5	4.8	4.7
99	6.4	6.1	5.9	5.6	5.4	5.2	5	4.9	4.7	4.5
100	6.3	6	5.8	5.5	5.3	5.1	4.9	4.7	4.5	4.4

Table II - Joint and Last Survivor Expectancy (cont.)

Ages	90	91	92	93	94	95	96	97	98	99
101	6.2	5.9	5.6	5.4	5.2	5	4.8	4.6	4.4	4.2
102	6.1	5.8	5.5	5.3	5.1	4.8	4.6	4.4	4.3	4.1
103	6	5.7	5.4	5.2	5	4.7	4.5	4.3	4.1	4
104	5.9	5.6	5.4	5.1	4.9	4.6	4.4	4.2	4	3.8
105	5.9	5.6	5.3	5	4.8	4.5	4.3	4.1	3.9	3.7
106	5.8	5.5	5.2	4.9	4.7	4.5	4.2	4	3.8	3.6
107	5.8	5.4	5.1	4.9	4.6	4.4	4.2	3.9	3.7	3.5
108	5.7	5.4	5.1	4.8	4.6	4.3	4.1	3.9	3.7	3.5
109	5.7	5.3	5	4.8	4.5	4.3	4	3.8	3.6	3.4
110	5.6	5.3	5	4.7	4.5	4.2	4	3.8	3.5	3.3
111	5.6	5.3	5	4.7	4.4	4.2	3.9	3.7	3.5	3.3
112	5.6	5.3	4.9	4.7	4.4	4.1	3.9	3.7	3.5	3.2
113	5.6	5.2	4.9	4.6	4.4	4.1	3.9	3.6	3.4	3.2
114	5.6	5.2	4.9	4.6	4.3	4.1	3.9	3.6	3.4	3.2
115+	5.5	5.2	4.9	4.6	4.3	4.1	3.8	3.6	3.4	3.1

Table III Uniform Lifetime Table

Age	Distribution Period	Age	Distribution Period
70	27.4	93	9.6
71	26.5	94	9.1
72	25.6	95	8.6
73	24.7	96	8.1
74	23.8	97	7.6
75	22.9	98	7.1
76	22.0	99	6.7
77	21.2	100	6.3
78	20.3	101	5.9
79	19.5	102	5.5
80	18.7	103	5.2
81	17.9	104	4.9
82	17.1	105	4.5
83	16.3	106	4.2
84	15.5	107	3.9
85	14.8	108	3.7
86	14.1	109	3.4
87	13.4	110	3.1
88	12.7	111	2.9
89	12.0	112	2.6
90	11.4	113	2.4
91	10.8	114	2.1
92	10.2	115 and over	1.9

Accredited Investors

Some alternative investments are only available to accredited investors and may have high account minimums to invest. Accredited investors are defined under the Securities Act of 1933 in Rule 501 of Regulation D[1] which states in part:

1. Any bank as defined in section 3(a)(2) of the Act, or any savings and loan association or other institution as defined in section 3(a)(5)(A) of the Act whether acting in its individual or fiduciary capacity; any broker or dealer registered pursuant to section 15 of the Securities Exchange Act of 1934; any insurance company as defined in section 2(a)(13) of the Act; any investment company registered under the Investment Company Act of 1940 or a business development company as defined in section 2(a)(48) of that Act; any Small Business Investment Company licensed by the U.S. Small Business Administration under section 301(c) or (d) of the Small Business Investment Act of 1958; any plan established and maintained by a state, its political subdivisions, or any agency or instrumentality of a state or its political subdivisions, for the benefit of its employees, if such plan has total assets in excess of $5,000,000; any employee benefit plan within the meaning of the Employee Retirement Income Security Act of 1974 if the investment decision is made by a plan fiduciary, as defined in section 3(21) of such act, which is either a bank, savings and loan association, insurance company, or registered investment adviser, or if the employee benefit plan has total assets in excess of $5,000,000 or, if a self-directed plan,

---

[1] 17 C.F.R. Section 230.501(a)

with investment decisions made solely by persons that are accredited investors;

2. Any private business development company as defined in section 202(a)(22) of the Investment Advisers Act of 1940;

3. Any organization described in section 501(c)(3) of the Internal Revenue Code, corporation, Massachusetts or similar business trust, or partnership, not formed for the specific purpose of acquiring the securities offered, with total assets in excess of $5,000,000;

4. Any director, executive officer, or general partner of the issuer of the securities being offered or sold, or any director, executive officer, or general partner of a general partner of that issuer;

5. Any natural person whose individual net worth, or joint net worth with that person's spouse, at the time of his purchase exceeds $1,000,000;

6. Any natural person who had an individual income in excess of $200,000 in each of the two most recent years or joint income with that person's spouse in excess of $300,000 in each of those years and has a reasonable expectation of reaching the same income level in the current year;

7. Any trust, with total assets in excess of $5,000,000, not formed for the specific purpose of acquiring the securities offered, whose purchase is directed by a sophisticated person as described in Rule 506(b)(2)(ii) and

8. Any entity in which all of the equity owners are accredited investors.

Note that item number five related to an individual person's net worth is currently under revision. The Dodd-Frank Wall Street Reform and Consumer Protection Act required the definition of accredited investor to be modified to exclude the value of a person's primary residence when determining their net worth. As of this writing, the SEC has issued proposed, but not final, language to make this rule change.

Additional Resources

Neither the author nor publisher are responsible for products, services, content or information available from the following third-party resources. They are provided as a courtesy to assist the reader in further information gathering. No endorsement is made or implied. The following lists are not intended to be exhaustive.

IRA Publication 590-IRAs
www.irs.gov

Private Investment Funds (PIFs)
Jagen™ Investments LLC, www.jagenfunds.com

Consulting/Training/Speaking Engagements
Jagen™ Investments LLC, www.jagenfunds.com

Self-Directed IRA Custodians:
Pensco Trust Company, www.pensco.com
Equity Trust Company, www.trustetc.com
Millennium Trust Company, www.mtrustcompany.com
Sterling Trust Company, www.sterling-trust.com
Provident Group, www.providentira.com
Lincoln Trust Company, www.lincolntrustco.com
Sunwest Trust Company, www.sunwesttrust.com
IRA Services Trust Company, www.iraservices.com
Self-Directed IRA Services, Inc., www.sdiraservices.com

Nonrecourse Loans:
North American Savings Bank, www.iralending.com
Island View Mortgage, www.islandviewmortgage.com
First Western Federal Savings Bank, www.myiralender.com
Lending Resources Group,
www.lendingresourcesgroup.com

Valuation Firms
Howard Frazier Barker Elliott, Inc., www.hfbe.com
FMV Opinions, Inc., www.fmv.com
Business Valuations, Ltd., www.bizvalsltd.com
Pluris Valuation Advisors LLC, www.pluris.com
Iron Horse Business Valuation Group, www.gibbspc.com

Social Media Connections

Website
www.KEEPITIRA.com
www.jagenfunds.com

Twitter
@JagenFunds

Facebook
www.facebook.com/pages/Jagen-Funds/197170653656602

LinkedIn
www.linkedin.com/company/jagen-investments-llc

Index

Symbols

401(k) 11, 11–20, 14, 152

A

accredited investor 41, 183
alternative assets 19, 64
annuities 14, 17, 41
appraisal 40, 53, 64, 77, 102, 141, 154, 156
appraiser 14, 30, 31, 32, 38, 40, 48, 102, 116, 141, 143
asset class segregation 71
author 192

B

bankruptcy 15, 27, 48, 151, 152, 153, 154, 155, 156
bonds 14, 17, 30, 41, 75, 126

C

capital gains 34, 75, 76, 77, 78, 79, 119, 131, 132, 144
CDs 14, 17, 75
charitable gift 95, 101, 132
collectibles 21, 34
cost basis 64, 77, 147, 154
creditor 15, 151, 155, 156
custodian 17, 19, 28, 51, 53, 75, 82, 109, 110, 112, 143, 154, 156

D

defined benefit plans 14,

defined contribution plan 11, 14
discount valuation 51, 52, 65, 69, 70, 83, 88, 92, 115, 125, 152

disqualified person 22, 23, 24, 25, 111, 112
DPP 61
discount valuation 51, 52, 65, 69, 70, 83, 88, 92, 115, 125

E

ERISA 152
estate tax 12, 27, 40, 48, 65, 91, 92, 95, 97, 98, 99, 132, 137, 138
ETFs 14, 30
excise tax 81

F

fair market value 14, 29
FINRA 61
Form 1099-R 28, 30, 51, 53, 63, 64, 75, 77, 82, 143
Form 5498 29, 65

G

gift tax 33

H

hedge funds 14, 43, 125

I

income tax 12, 51, 52, 54, 57, 58, 63, 76, 77, 81, 85, 92, 97, 98, 99, 110, 119, 138, 139, 144, 145
inflation 152
Internal Revenue Manual 28, 29, 102
interval funds 14
Investment Company Institute 11

Acknowledgments

As with any significant endeavor, many people were involved with bringing this book project to fruition. My sincere gratitude for their time, input, encouragement, talents and knowledge knows no bounds. Many are friends and colleagues that are too numerous to name as I have learned from some of the best in the industry. Others were in the trenches with me throughout the process.

First and most of all, I must thank my right hand woman, Lauren Gabourel. Lauren has been my personal assistant for over six years and is irreplaceable. This book would not exist if not for her, period. She finally bugged me enough to actually write it, and it's only been about five years in coming! She also encouraged me throughout the process, forced me to work on it when I wanted to put it off and demanded my attention to things like cover design when necessary. Lauren also handled one hundred percent of the layout work, designed the cover front and back and provided invaluable input on style, marketing and more. Thank you Lauren!

Next is trust development officer Kevin Mooney in Reno, Nevada. Kevin and I worked together for a long time traipsing around the country to the point where our lives felt like one long tax conference according to Kevin. And I concurred. He was an early reviewer of the text providing excellent content suggestions. He remains a partner in the Jagen™ family of companies and one of my favorite business confidants.

Attorney Craig Stone has been a close business associate for as long as I've been in Nevada. Craig has been instrumental in the development of some of the ideas presented in this book as well as the Jagen™ investment philosophies. I rely on his counsel for more matters than I can count and am thankful for his sage advice and friendship.

Thanks also to IRA and ERISA attorney par excellence Ami Givon in San Francisco. Ami has been our exclusive ERISA counsel for many years, and he was kind enough to provide invaluable input and suggestions for this book. Also providing excellent commentary and support for this text was Tom Anderson, founder of PENSCO Trust Company and current president of the Retirement Industry Trust Association (RITA). Tom has forgotten more about IRA rules, regulations and transactions than most of us will ever know.

I also owe great thanks to my other partners in the Jagen™ family of companies who believed in me and the ideas in this book long before anyone else. Their continued support and encouragement are the fuel that keeps me going.

And last, but first, to God for giving me the ability to pursue this endeavor which I have most enjoyed. Hopefully, I have used His gifts well to present technical information in an easy to understand format as was my goal.

About The Author

Joe Luby is the founder of the Jagen™ family of companies. The Jagen™ designed private investment fund is a unique development in the planning field offering significant investment opportunities combined with tax efficiencies for clients with large IRAs and/or gift and estate tax concerns.

A highly regarded and effective speaker, Mr. Luby travels extensively speaking at national events educating the country's top professionals on advanced planning topics. He consults for other professional advisors in the area of valuation adjustment strategies and opportunities including tax benefits inherent in the design and operation of many alternative investment vehicles such as hedge funds, private REITs, etc. Mr. Luby also consults on advanced planning strategies for large IRAs and estates.

Mr. Luby holds the Certified Financial Planner™ designation. Prior to founding Jagen™, he owned and operated a high end financial planning firm with a primary focus on wealth management and preservation strategies. He is an established expert in the areas of charitable gift planning, advanced corporate retirement plan design and management, alternative investment transactions using retirement funds and the special needs of successful business owners including advanced tax and estate planning strategies.

To inquire about speaking and/or consulting engagements, please visit www.jagenfunds.com or email info@jagenfunds.com.